The Pelican Shakespeare
General Editors

STEPHEN ORGEL
A. R. BRAUNMULLER

Love's Labor's Lost

The comedian Thomas Weston (1737–1776) as Costard in
Garrick's production of *Love's Labor's Lost* at Drury Lane.
From Bell's Shakespeare, 1776.

William Shakespeare

———

Love's Labor's Lost

EDITED BY PETER HOLLAND

PENGUIN BOOKS

PENGUIN BOOKS
Published by the Penguin Group
Penguin Putnam Inc., 375 Hudson Street,
New York, New York 10014, U.S.A.
Penguin Books Ltd, 27 Wrights Lane,
London W8 5TZ, England
Penguin Books Australia Ltd, Ringwood,
Victoria, Australia
Penguin Books Canada Ltd, 10 Alcorn Avenue,
Toronto, Ontario, Canada M4V 3B2
Penguin Books (N.Z.) Ltd, 182–190 Wairau Road,
Auckland 10, New Zealand

Penguin Books Ltd, Registered Offices:
Harmondsworth, Middlesex, England

Love's Labor's Lost edited by Alfred Harbage published in the
United States of America in Penguin Books 1963
Revised edition published 1973
This new edition edited by Peter Holland published 2000

1 3 5 7 9 10 8 6 4 2

Copyright © Penguin Books Inc., 1963, 1973
Copyright © Penguin Putnam Inc., 2000
All rights reserved

ISBN 0-14-07.1477 4
(CIP data available)

Printed in the United States of America
Set in Adobe Garamond
Designed by Virginia Norey

Contents

Publisher's Note

IT IS ALMOST half a century since the first volumes of the Pelican Shakespeare appeared under the general editorship of Alfred Harbage. The fact that a new edition, rather than simply a revision, has been undertaken reflects the profound changes textual and critical studies of Shakespeare have undergone in the past twenty years. For the new Pelican series, the texts of the plays and poems have been thoroughly revised in accordance with recent scholarship, and in some cases have been entirely reedited. New introductions and notes have been provided in all the volumes. But the new Shakespeare is also designed as a successor to the original series; the previous editions have been taken into account, and the advice of the previous editors has been solicited where it was feasible to do so.

Certain textual features of the new Pelican Shakespeare should be particularly noted. All lines are numbered that contain a word, phrase, or allusion explained in the glossarial notes. In addition, for convenience, every tenth line is also numbered, in italics when no annotation is indicated. The intrusive and often inaccurate place headings inserted by early editors are omitted (as is becoming standard practice), but for the convenience of those who miss them, an indication of locale now appears as the first item in the annotation of each scene.

In the interest of both elegance and utility, each speech prefix is set in a separate line when the speaker's lines are in verse, except when those words form the second half of a verse line. Thus the verse form of the speech is kept visually intact. What is printed as verse and what is printed as prose has, in general, the authority of the original texts. Departures from the original texts in this regard have only the authority of editorial tradition and the judgment of the Pelican editors; and, in a few instances, are admittedly arbitrary.

The Theatrical World

ECONOMIC REALITIES determined the theatrical world in which Shakespeare's plays were written, performed, and received. For centuries in England, the primary theatrical tradition was nonprofessional. Craft guilds (or "mysteries") provided religious drama – mystery plays – as part of the celebration of religious and civic festivals, and schools and universities staged classical and neoclassical drama in both Latin and English as part of their curricula. In these forms, drama was established and socially acceptable. Professional theater, in contrast, existed on the margins of society. The acting companies were itinerant; playhouses could be any available space – the great halls of the aristocracy, town squares, civic halls, inn yards, fair booths, or open fields – and income was sporadic, dependent on the passing of the hat or on the bounty of local patrons. The actors, moreover, were considered little better than vagabonds, constantly in danger of arrest or expulsion.

In the late 1560s and 1570s, however, English professional theater began to gain respectability. Wealthy aristocrats fond of drama – the Lord Admiral, for example, or the Lord Chamberlain – took acting companies under their protection so that the players technically became members of their households and were no longer subject to arrest as homeless or masterless men. Permanent theaters were first built at this time as well, allowing the companies to control and charge for entry to their performances.

Shakespeare's livelihood, and the stunning artistic explosion in which he participated, depended on pragmatic and architectural effort. Professional theater requires ways to restrict access to its offerings; if it does not, and admission fees cannot be charged, the actors do not get paid, the costumes go to a pawnbroker, and there is no such thing as a professional, ongoing theatrical tradition. The answer to that economic need arrived in the late 1560s and 1570s with the creation of the so-called public or amphitheater playhouse. Recent discoveries indicate that the precursor of the Globe playhouse in London (where Shakespeare's mature plays were presented) and the Rose theater (which presented Christopher Marlowe's plays and some of Shakespeare's earliest ones) was the Red Lion theater of 1567. Archaeological studies of the foundations of the Rose and Globe theaters have revealed that the open-air theater of the 1590s and later was probably a polygonal building with fourteen to twenty or twenty-four sides, multistoried, from 75 to 100 feet in diameter, with a raised, partly covered "thrust" stage that projected into a group of standing patrons, or "groundlings," and a covered gallery, seating up to 2,500 or more (very crowded) spectators.

These theaters might have been about half full on any given day, though the audiences were larger on holidays or when a play was advertised, as old and new were, through printed playbills posted around London. The metropolitan area's late-Tudor, early-Stuart population (circa 1590-1620) has been estimated at about 150,000 to 250,000. It has been supposed that in the mid-1590s there were about 15,000 spectators per week at the public theaters; thus, as many as 10 percent of the local population went to the theater regularly. Consequently, the theaters' repertories – the plays available for this experienced and frequent audience – had to change often: in the month between September 15 and October 15, 1595, for instance, the Lord Admiral's Men performed twenty-eight times in eighteen different plays.

Since natural light illuminated the amphitheaters' stages, performances began between noon and two o'clock and ran without a break for two or three hours. They often concluded with a jig, a fencing display, or some other nondramatic exhibition. Weather conditions determined the season for the amphitheaters: plays were performed every day (including Sundays, sometimes, to clerical dismay) except during Lent – the forty days before Easter – or periods of plague, or sometimes during the summer months when law courts were not in session and the most affluent members of the audience were not in London.

To a modern theatergoer, an amphitheater stage like that of the Rose or Globe would appear an unfamiliar mixture of plainness and elaborate decoration. Much of the structure was carved or painted, sometimes to imitate marble; elsewhere, as under the canopy projecting over the stage, to represent the stars and the zodiac. Appropriate painted canvas pictures (of Jerusalem, for example, if the play was set in that city) were apparently hung on the wall behind the acting area, and tragedies were accompanied by black hangings, presumably something like crepe festoons or bunting. Although these theaters did not employ what we would call scenery, early modern spectators saw numerous large props, such as the "bar" at which a prisoner stood during a trial, the "mossy bank" where lovers reclined, an arbor for amorous conversation, a chariot, gallows, tables, trees, beds, thrones, writing desks, and so forth. Audiences might learn a scene's location from a sign (reading "Athens," for example) carried across the stage (as in Bertolt Brecht's twentieth-century productions). Equally captivating (and equally irritating to the theater's enemies) were the rich costumes and personal props the actors used: the most valuable items in the surviving theatrical inventories are the swords, gowns, robes, crowns, and other items worn or carried by the performers.

Magic appealed to Shakespeare's audiences as much as it does to us today, and the theater exploited many deceptive and spectacular devices. A winch in the loft above the stage, called "the heavens," could lower and raise actors playing gods, goddesses, and other supernatural figures to and from the main acting area, just as one or more trapdoors permitted entrances and exits to and from the area, called "hell," beneath the stage. Actors wore elementary makeup such as wigs, false beards, and face paint, and they employed pig's bladders filled with animal blood to make wounds seem more real. They had rudimentary but effective ways of pretending to behead or hang a person. Supernumeraries (stagehands or actors not needed in a particular scene) could make thunder sounds (by shaking a metal sheet or rolling an iron ball down a chute) and show lightning (by blowing inflammable resin through tubes into a flame). Elaborate fireworks enhanced the effects of dragons flying through the air or imitated such celestial phenomena as comets, shooting stars, and multiple suns. Horses' hoofbeats, bells (located perhaps in the tower above the stage), trumpets and drums, clocks, cannon shots and gunshots, and the like were common sound effects. And the music of viols, cornets, oboes, and recorders was a regular feature of theatrical performances.

For two relatively brief spans, from the late 1570s to 1590 and from 1599 to 1614, the amphitheaters competed with the so-called private, or indoor, theaters, which originated as, or later represented themselves as, educational institutions training boys as singers for church services and court performances. These indoor theaters had two features that were distinct from the amphitheaters': their personnel and their playing spaces. The amphitheaters' adult companies included both adult men, who played the male roles, and boys, who played the female roles; the private, or indoor, theater companies, on the other hand, were entirely composed of boys aged about 8 to 16, who were, or could pretend to be, candidates for singers in a church or a royal boys' choir. (Until 1660, professional theatrical companies included no women.) The playing space would appear much more familiar to modern audiences than the long-vanished amphitheaters; the later indoor theaters were, in fact, the ancestors of the typical modern theater. They were enclosed spaces, usually rectangular, with the stage filling one end of the rectangle and the audience arrayed in seats or benches across (and sometimes lining) the building's longer axis. These spaces staged plays less frequently than the public theaters (perhaps only once a week) and held far fewer spectators than the amphitheaters: about 200 to 600, as opposed to 2,500 or more. Fewer patrons mean a smaller gross income, unless each pays more. Not surprisingly, then, private theaters charged higher prices than the amphitheaters, probably sixpence, as opposed to a penny for the cheapest entry.

Protected from the weather, the indoor theaters presented plays later in the day than the amphitheaters, and used artificial illumination – candles in sconces or candelabra. But candles melt, and need replacing, snuffing, and trimming, and these practical requirements may have been part of the reason the indoor theaters introduced breaks in the performance, the intermission so dear to the heart of theatergoers and to the pocketbooks of theater concessionaires ever since. Whether motivated by the need to tend to the candles or by the entrepreneurs' wishing to sell oranges and liquor, or both, the indoor theaters eventually established the modern convention of the non-continuous performance. In the early modern "private" theater, musical performances apparently filled the intermissions, which in Stuart theater jargon seem to have been called "acts."

At the end of the first decade of the seventeenth century, the distinction between public amphitheaters and private indoor companies ceased. For various cultural, political, and economic reasons, individual companies gained control of both the public, open-air theaters and the indoor ones, and companies mixing adult men and boys took over the formerly "private" theaters. Despite the death of the boys' companies and of their highly innovative theaters (for which such luminous playwrights as Ben Jonson, George Chapman, and John Marston wrote), their playing spaces and conventions had an immense impact on subsequent plays: not merely for the intervals (which stressed the artistic and architectonic importance of "acts"), but also because they introduced political and social satire as a popular dramatic ingredient, even in tragedy, and a wider range of actorly effects, encouraged by their more intimate playing spaces.

Even the briefest sketch of the Shakespearean theatrical world would be incomplete without some comment on the social and cultural dimensions of theaters and playing in the period. In an intensely hierarchical and status-conscious society, professional actors and their ventures had hardly any respectability; as we have indicated, to protect themselves against laws designed to curb vagabondage and the increase of masterless men, actors resorted to the near-fiction that they were the servants of noble masters, and wore their distinctive livery. Hence the company for which Shakespeare wrote in the 1590s called itself the Lord Chamberlain's Men and pretended that the public, money-getting performances were in fact rehearsals for private performances before that high court official. From 1598, the Privy Council had licensed theatrical companies, and after 1603, with the accession of King James I, the companies gained explicit royal protection, just as the Queen's Men had for a time under Queen Elizabeth. The Chamberlain's Men became the King's Men, and the other companies were patronized by the other members of the royal family.

These designations were legal fictions that half-concealed an important economic and social development, the evolution away from the theater's organization on the model of the guild, a self-regulating confraternity of individual artisans, into a proto-capitalist organization. Shakespeare's company became a joint-stock company, where persons who supplied capital and, in some cases, such as Shakespeare's, capital and talent, employed themselves and others in earning a return on that capital. This development meant that actors and theater companies were outside both the traditional guild structures, which required some form of civic or royal charter, and the feudal household organization of master-and-servant. This anomalous, maverick social and economic condition made theater companies practically unruly and potentially even dangerous; consequently, numerous official bodies – including the London metropolitan and ecclesiastical authorities as well as, occasionally, the royal court itself – tried, without much success, to control and even to disband them.

Public officials had good reason to want to close the theaters: they were attractive nuisances – they drew often riotous crowds, they were always noisy, and they could be politically offensive and socially insubordinate. Until the Civil War, however, anti-theatrical forces failed to shut down professional theater, for many reasons – limited surveillance and few police powers, tensions or outright hostilities among the agencies that sought to check or channel theatrical activity, and lack of clear policies for control. Another reason must have been the theaters' undeniable popularity. Curtailing any activity enjoyed by such a substantial percentage of the population was difficult, as various Roman emperors attempting to limit circuses had learned, and the Tudor-Stuart audience was not merely large, it was socially diverse and included women. The prevalence of public entertainment in this period has been underestimated. In fact, fairs, holidays, games, sporting events, the equivalent of modern parades, freak shows, and street exhibitions all abounded, but the theater was the most widely and frequently available entertainment to which people of every class had access. That fact helps account both for its quantity and for the fear and anger it aroused.

WILLIAM SHAKESPEARE OF STRATFORD-UPON-AVON, GENTLEMAN

Many people have said that we know very little about William Shakespeare's life – pinheads and postcards are often mentioned as appropriately tiny surfaces on which to record the available information. More imaginatively and perhaps more correctly, Ralph Waldo Emerson wrote, "Shakespeare is the only biographer of Shakespeare. . . . So far from Shakespeare's being the least known, he is the one person in all modern history fully known to us."

In fact, we know more about Shakespeare's life than we do about almost any other English writer's of his era. His last will and testament (dated March 25, 1616) survives, as do numerous legal contracts and court documents involving Shakespeare as principal or witness, and parish records in Stratford and London. Shakespeare appears quite often in official records of King James's royal court, and of course Shakespeare's name appears on numerous title pages and in the written and recorded words of his literary contemporaries Robert Greene, Henry Chettle, Francis Meres, John Davies of Hereford, Ben Jonson, and many others. Indeed, if we make due allowance for the bloating of modern, run-of-the-mill bureaucratic records, more information has survived over the past four hundred years about William Shakespeare of Stratford-upon-Avon, Warwickshire, than is likely to survive in the next four hundred years about any reader of these words.

What we do not have are entire categories of information – Shakespeare's private letters or diaries, drafts and revisions of poems and plays, critical prefaces or essays, commendatory verse for other writers' works, or instructions guiding his fellow actors in their performances, for instance – that we imagine would help us understand and appreciate his surviving writings. For all we know, many such data never existed as written records. Many literary and theatrical critics, not knowing what might once have existed, more or less cheerfully accept the situation; some even make a theoretical virtue of it by claiming that such data are irrelevant to understanding and interpreting the plays and poems.

So, what do we know about William Shakespeare, the man responsible for thirty-seven or perhaps more plays, more than 150 sonnets, two lengthy narrative poems, and some shorter poems?

While many families by the name of Shakespeare (or some variant spelling) can be identified in the English Midlands as far back as the twelfth century, it seems likely that the dramatist's grandfather, Richard, moved to Snitterfield, a town not far from Stratford-upon-Avon, sometime before 1529. In Snitterfield, Richard Shakespeare leased farmland from the very wealthy Robert Arden. By 1552, Richard's son John had moved to a large house on Henley Street in Stratford-upon-Avon, the house that stands today as "The Birthplace." In Stratford, John Shakespeare traded as a glover, dealt in wool, and lent money at interest; he also served in a variety of civic posts, including "High Bailiff," the municipality's equivalent of mayor. In 1557, he married Robert Arden's youngest daughter, Mary. Mary and John had four sons – William was the oldest – and four daughters, of whom only Joan outlived her most celebrated sibling. William was baptized (an event entered in the Stratford parish church records) on April 26, 1564, and it has become customary, without any good factual support, to suppose he was born on April 23, which happens to be the feast day of Saint George, patron saint of England, and is also the date on which he died, in 1616. Shakespeare married Anne Hathaway in 1582, when he was eighteen and she was twenty-six; their first child was born five months later. It has been generally assumed that the marriage was enforced and subsequently unhappy, but these are only assumptions; it has been estimated, for instance, that up to one third of Elizabethan brides were pregnant when they married. Anne and William Shakespeare had three children: Susanna, who married a prominent local physician, John Hall; and the twins Hamnet, who died young in 1596, and Judith, who married Thomas Quiney – apparently a rather shady individual. The name Hamnet was unusual but not unique: he and his twin sister were named for their godparents, Shakespeare's neighbors Hamnet and Judith Sadler. Shakespeare's father died in 1601 (the year of *Hamlet*), and Mary Arden Shakespeare died in 1608 (the year of *Coriolanus*). William Shakespeare's last surviving direct descendant was his granddaughter Elizabeth Hall, who died in 1670.

Between the birth of the twins in 1585 and a clear reference to Shakespeare as a practicing London dramatist in Robert Greene's sensationalizing, satiric pamphlet, *Greene's Groatsworth of Wit* (1592), there is no record of where William Shakespeare was or what he was doing. These seven so-called lost years have been imaginatively filled by scholars and other students of Shakespeare: some think he traveled to Italy, or fought in the Low Countries, or studied law or medicine, or worked as an apprentice actor/writer, and so on to even more fanciful possibilities. Whatever the biographical facts for those "lost" years, Greene's nasty remarks in 1592 testify to professional envy and to the fact that Shakespeare already had a successful career in London. Speaking to his fellow playwrights, Greene warns both generally and specifically:

> . . . trust them [actors] not: for there is an upstart crow, beautified with our feathers, that with his tiger's heart wrapped in a player's hide supposes he is as well able to bombast out a blank verse as the best of you; and being an absolute Johannes Factotum, is in his own conceit the only Shake-scene in a country.

The passage mimics a line from *3 Henry VI* (hence the play must have been performed before Greene wrote) and seems to say that "Shake-scene" is both actor and playwright, a jack-of-all-trades. That same year, Henry Chettle protested Greene's remarks in *Kind-Heart's Dream,* and each of the next two years saw the publication of poems – *Venus and Adonis* and *The Rape of Lucrece,* respectively – publicly ascribed to (and dedicated by) Shakespeare. Early in 1595 he was named one of the senior members of a prominent acting company, the Lord Chamberlain's Men, when they received payment for court performances during the 1594 Christmas season.

Clearly, Shakespeare had achieved both success and reputation in London. In 1596, upon Shakespeare's application, the College of Arms granted his father the now-familiar coat of arms he had taken the first steps to obtain almost twenty years before, and in 1598, John's son – now permitted to call himself "gentleman" – took a 10 percent share in the new Globe playhouse. In 1597, he bought a substantial bourgeois house, called New Place, in Stratford – the garden remains, but Shakespeare's house, several times rebuilt, was torn down in 1759 – and over the next few years Shakespeare spent large sums buying land and making other investments in the town and its environs. Though he worked in London, his family remained in Stratford, and he seems always to have considered Stratford the home he would eventually return to. Something approaching a disinterested appreciation of Shakespeare's popular and professional status appears in Francis Meres's *Palladis Tamia* (1598), a not especially imaginative and perhaps therefore persuasive record of literary reputations. Reviewing contemporary English writers, Meres lists the titles of many of Shakespeare's plays, including one not now known, *Love's Labor's Won*, and praises his "mellifluous & hony-tongued" "sugred Sonnets," which were then circulating in manuscript (they were first collected in 1609). Meres describes Shakespeare as "one of the best" English playwrights of both comedy and tragedy. In *Remains . . . Concerning Britain* (1605), William Camden – a more authoritative source than the imitative Meres – calls Shakespeare one of the "most pregnant witts of these our times" and joins him with such writers as Chapman, Daniel, Jonson, Marston, and Spenser. During the first decades of the seventeenth century, publishers began to attribute numerous play quartos, including some non-Shakespearean ones, to Shakespeare, either by name or initials, and we may assume that they deemed Shakespeare's name and supposed authorship, true or false, commercially attractive.

For the next ten years or so, various records show

Shakespeare's dual career as playwright and man of the theater in London, and as an important local figure in Stratford. In 1608-9 his acting company – designated the "King's Men" soon after King James had succeeded Queen Elizabeth in 1603 – rented, refurbished, and opened a small interior playing space, the Blackfriars theater, in London, and Shakespeare was once again listed as a substantial sharer in the group of proprietors of the playhouse. By May 11, 1612, however, he describes himself as a Stratford resident in a London lawsuit – an indication that he had withdrawn from day-to-day professional activity and returned to the town where he had always had his main financial interests. When Shakespeare bought a substantial residential building in London, the Blackfriars Gatehouse, close to the theater of the same name, on March 10, 1613, he is recorded as William Shakespeare "of Stratford upon Avon in the county of Warwick, gentleman," and he named several London residents as the building's trustees. Still, he continued to participate in theatrical activity: when the new Earl of Rutland needed an allegorical design to bear as a shield, or *impresa,* at the celebration of King James's Accession Day, March 24, 1613, the earl's accountant recorded a payment of 44 shillings to Shakespeare for the device with its motto.

For the last few years of his life, Shakespeare evidently concentrated his activities in the town of his birth. Most of the final records concern business transactions in Stratford, ending with the notation of his death on April 23, 1616, and burial in Holy Trinity Church, Stratford-upon-Avon.

THE QUESTION OF AUTHORSHIP

The history of ascribing Shakespeare's plays (the poems do not come up so often) to someone else began, as it continues, peculiarly. The earliest published claim that someone else wrote Shakespeare's plays appeared in an 1856 article by Delia Bacon in the American journal *Putnam's Monthly* – although an Englishman, Thomas Wilmot, had shared his doubts in private (even secretive) conversations with friends near the end of the eighteenth century. Bacon's was a sad personal history that ended in madness and poverty, but the year after her article, she published, with great difficulty and the bemused assistance of Nathaniel Hawthorne (then United States Consul in Liverpool, England), her *Philosophy of the Plays of Shakspere Unfolded*. This huge, ornately written, confusing farrago is almost unreadable; sometimes its intents, to say nothing of its arguments, disappear entirely beneath near-raving, ecstatic writing. Tumbled in with much supposed "philosophy" appear the claims that Francis Bacon (from whom Delia Bacon eventually claimed descent), Walter Ralegh, and several other contemporaries of Shakespeare's had written the plays. The book had little impact except as a ridiculed curiosity.

Once proposed, however, the issue gained momentum among people whose conviction was the greater in proportion to their ignorance of sixteenth- and seventeenth-century English literature, history, and society. Another American amateur, Catherine P. Ashmead Windle, made the next influential contribution to the cause when she published *Report to the British Museum* (1882), wherein she promised to open "the Cipher of Francis Bacon," though what she mostly offers, in the words of S. Schoenbaum, is "demented allegorizing." An entire new cottage industry grew from Windle's suggestion that the texts contain hidden, cryptographically discoverable ciphers – "clues" – to their authorship; and today there are not only books devoted to the putative ciphers, but also pamphlets, journals, and newsletters.

Although Baconians have led the pack of those seeking a substitute Shakespeare, in *"Shakespeare" Identified* (1920), J. Thomas Looney became the first published

"Oxfordian" when he proposed Edward de Vere, seven-teenth earl of Oxford, as the secret author of Shakespeare's plays. Also for Oxford and his "authorship" there are today dedicated societies, articles, journals, and books. Less popular candidates – Queen Elizabeth and Christo-pher Marlowe among them – have had adherents, but the movement seems to have divided into two main contend-ing factions, Baconian and Oxfordian. (For further details on all the candidates for "Shakespeare," see S. Schoen-baum, *Shakespeare's Lives,* 2nd ed., 1991.)

The Baconians, the Oxfordians, and supporters of other candidates have one trait in common – they are snobs. Every pro-Bacon or pro-Oxford tract sooner or later claims that the historical William Shakespeare of Stratford-upon-Avon could not have written the plays be-cause he could not have had the training, the university education, the experience, and indeed the imagination or background their author supposedly possessed. Only a learned genius like Bacon or an aristocrat like Oxford could have written such fine plays. (As it happens, lucky male children of the middle class had access to better edu-cation than most aristocrats in Elizabethan England – and Oxford was not particularly well educated.) Shake-speare received in the Stratford grammar school a formal education that would daunt many college graduates today; and popular rival playwrights such as the very learned Ben Jonson and George Chapman, both of whom also lacked university training, achieved great artistic suc-cess, without being taken as Bacon or Oxford.

Besides snobbery, one other quality characterizes the authorship controversy: lack of evidence. A great deal of testimony from Shakespeare's time shows that Shake-speare wrote Shakespeare's plays and that his contempo-raries recognized them as distinctive and distinctly superior. (Some of that contemporary evidence is col-lected in E. K. Chambers, *William Shakespeare: A Study of Facts and Problems,* 2 vols., 1930.) Since that testimony comes from Shakespeare's enemies and theatrical competitors as well as from his co-workers and from the Elizabethan equivalent of literary journalists, it seems unlikely that, if any one of these sources had known he was a fraud, they would have failed to record that fact.

Books About Shakespeare's Theater

Useful scholarly studies of theatrical life in Shakespeare's day include: G. E. Bentley, *The Jacobean and Caroline Stage,* 7 vols. (1941-68), and the same author's *The Professions of Dramatist and Player in Shakespeare's Time, 1590-1642* (1986); E. K. Chambers, *The Elizabethan Stage,* 4 vols. (1923); R. A. Foakes, *Illustrations of the English Stage, 1580-1642* (1985); Andrew Gurr, *The Shakespearean Stage,* 3rd ed. (1992), and the same author's *Play-going in Shakespeare's London,* 2nd ed. (1996); Edwin Nungezer, *A Dictionary of Actors* (1929); Carol Chillington Rutter, ed., *Documents of the Rose Playhouse* (1984).

Books About Shakespeare's Life

The following books provide scholarly, documented accounts of Shakespeare's life: G. E. Bentley, *Shakespeare: A Biographical Handbook* (1961); E. K. Chambers, *William Shakespeare: A Study of Facts and Problems,* 2 vols. (1930); S. Schoenbaum, *William Shakespeare: A Compact Documentary Life* (1977); and *Shakespeare's Lives,* 2nd ed. (1991), by the same author. Many scholarly editions of Shakespeare's complete works print brief compilations of essential dates and events. References to Shakespeare's works up to 1700 are collected in C. M. Ingleby et al., *The Shakespeare Allusion-Book,* rev. ed., 2 vols. (1932).

The Texts of Shakespeare

As far as we know, only one manuscript conceivably in Shakespeare's own hand may (and even this is much disputed) exist: a few pages of a play called *Sir Thomas More,* which apparently was never performed. What we do have, as later readers, performers, scholars, students, are printed texts. The earliest of these survive in two forms: quartos and folios. Quartos (from the Latin for "four") are small books, printed on sheets of paper that were then folded in fours, to make eight double-sided pages. When these were bound together, the result was a squarish, eminently portable volume that sold for the relatively small sum of sixpence (translating in modern terms to about $5.00). In folios, on the other hand, the sheets are folded only once, in half, producing large, impressive volumes taller than they are wide. This was the format for important works of philosophy, science, theology, and literature (the major precedent for a folio Shakespeare was Ben Jonson's *Works,* 1616). The decision to print the works of a popular playwright in folio is an indication of how far up on the social scale the theatrical profession had come during Shakespeare's lifetime. The Shakespeare folio was an expensive book, selling for between fifteen and eighteen shillings, depending on the binding (in modern terms, from about $150 to $180). Twenty Shakespeare plays of the thirty-seven that survive first appeared in quarto, seventeen of which appeared during Shakespeare's lifetime; the rest of the plays are found only in folio.

The First Folio was published in 1623, seven years after Shakespeare's death, and was authorized by his fellow actors, the co-owners of the King's Men. This publication was certainly a mark of the company's enormous respect for Shakespeare; but it was also a way of turning the old plays, most of which were no longer current in the play-house, into ready money (the folio includes only Shake-speare's plays, not his sonnets or other nondramatic verse). Whatever the motives behind the publication of the folio, the texts it preserves constitute the basis for almost all later editions of the playwright's works. The texts, however, differ from those of the earlier quartos, sometimes in minor respects but often significantly – most strikingly in the two texts of *King Lear,* but also in important ways in *Hamlet, Othello,* and *Troilus and Cressida.* (The variants are recorded in the textual notes to each play in the new Pelican series.) The differences in these texts represent, in a sense, the essence of theater: the texts of plays were initially not intended for publication. They were scripts, designed for the actors to perform – the principal life of the play at this period was in performance. And it follows that in Shakespeare's theater the playwright typically had no say either in how his play was performed or in the disposition of his text – he was an employee of the company. The authoritative figures in the theatrical enterprise were the shareholders in the company, who were for the most part the major actors. They decided what plays were to be done; they hired the playwright and often gave him an outline of the play they wanted him to write. Often, too, the play was a collaboration: the company would retain a group of writers, and parcel out the scenes among them. The resulting script was then the property of the company, and the actors would revise it as they saw fit during the course of putting it on stage. The resulting text belonged to the company. The playwright had no rights in it once he had been paid. (This system survives largely intact in the movie industry, and most of the playwrights of Shakespeare's time were as anonymous as most screenwriters are today.) The script could also, of course, continue to change as the tastes of audiences and the requirements of the actors changed. Many – perhaps most – plays were revised when they were reintroduced after any substantial absence from the repertory, or when they were performed

by a company different from the one that originally com-
missioned the play.

Shakespeare was an exceptional figure in this world
because he was not only a shareholder and actor in his
company, but also its leading playwright – he was literally
his own boss. He had, moreover, little interest in the
publication of his plays, and even those that appeared
during his lifetime with the authorization of the company
show no signs of any editorial concern on the part of
the author. Theater was, for Shakespeare, a fluid and
supremely responsive medium – the very opposite of the
great classic canonical text that has embodied his works
since 1623.

The very fluidity of the original texts, however, has
meant that Shakespeare has always had to be edited. Here
is an example of how problematic the editorial project inevitably is, a passage from the most famous speech in
Romeo and Juliet, Juliet's balcony soliloquy beginning "O
Romeo, Romeo, wherefore art thou Romeo?" Since the
eighteenth century, the standard modern text has read,

> What's Montague? It is nor hand, nor foot,
> Nor arm, nor face, nor any other part
> Belonging to a man. O be some other name!
> What's in a name? That which we call a rose
> By any other name would smell as sweet.
>
> (II.2.40-44)

Editors have three early texts of this play to work from,
two quarto texts and the folio. Here is how the First
Quarto (1597) reads:

> Whats *Mountague*? It is nor hand nor foote,
> Nor arme, nor face, nor any other part.
> Whats in a name? That which we call a Rofe,
> By any other name would fmell as fweet:

Here is the Second Quarto (1599):

> Whats *Mountague?* it is nor hand nor foote,
> Nor arme nor face, ô be some other name
> Belonging to a man.
> Whats in a name that which we call a rose,
> By any other word would smell as sweete,

And here is the First Folio (1623):

> What's *Mountague?* it is nor hand nor foote,
> Nor arme, nor face, O be some other name
> Belonging to a man.
> What? in a names that which we call a Rose,
> By any other word would smell as sweete,

There is in fact no early text that reads as our modern text does – and this is the most famous speech in the play. Instead, we have three quite different texts, all of which are clearly some version of the same speech, but none of which seems to us a final or satisfactory version. The transcendently beautiful passage in modern editions is an editorial invention: editors have succeeded in conflating and revising the three versions into something we recognize as great poetry. Is this what Shakespeare "really" wrote? Who can say? What we can say is that Shakespeare always had performance, not a book, in mind.

Books About the Shakespeare Texts

The standard study of the printing history of the First Folio is W. W. Greg, *The Shakespeare First Folio* (1955). J. K. Walton, *The Quarto Copy for the First Folio of Shakespeare* (1971), is a useful survey of the relation of the quartos to the folio. The second edition of Charlton Hinman's *Norton Facsimile* of the First Folio (1996), with a new introduction by Peter Blayney, is indispensable. Stanley Wells and Gary Taylor, *William Shakespeare: A Textual Companion,* keyed to the Oxford text, gives a comprehensive survey of the editorial situation for all the plays and poems.

THE GENERAL EDITORS

Introduction

THE CONTRASTING SONGS of Spring and Winter that are sung at the end of *Love's Labor's Lost* are, as Don Armado puts it, "maintained" (V.2.875) by two birds, the cuckoo and the owl. The owl's cry has in English long been represented as "Tu-whit, tu-who!" (902, 911) but, in the context of this play, where language seems always to be stretching after other, punning meanings, the bird's call seems no longer quite so innocent. It may be calling "to it," an encouragement to have sex (for, as King Lear will remind us, birds, as well as bees, do it: "the wren goes to't," IV.6.112). But it may also be asking "to who?": with whom can one go to it? It may be a statement about the play so far: there has been *too* much *wit, too* much *woo*ing. Now, in the play's final confrontation, with the death of the King of France, the wit games of wooing that the men have been playing take on a different perspective and a new urgency, in which wit no longer seems as valuable a commodity and has certainly proved to be singularly ineffective in persuading the women of the men's sincerity. Perhaps the men have been *too wit*ty to be able *to woo* effectively, for the women have taken their wooing only as "courtship, pleasant jest, and courtesy" (770); the word "courtship" itself has proved to be a contradictory pun, for while the men have been courting the women, seeking to form those relationships of couples that progress toward marriage, the women have understood it in a contrary sense, simply as "courtliness," the enjoyable but insubstantial forms of court behavior. Even the name of the owl itself has already in the play taken on some of these resonances of extensive punning, for when Boyet ends his repartee with Costard and Maria with the exit line "Good night, my good owl" (IV.1.140), he may be using a probable Elizabethan pronunciation of "owl" as "ole," thereby punning on "hole" and continuing the sexual jokes that had led Maria to reprimand both men: "you talk greasily; your lips grow foul" (IV.1.138).

If playing games with the possibilities that inhere in the owl's set of sounds transliterated into English seems only one more stage in the play's endless games with language, some of these games have by the end of *Love's Labor's Lost* begun to be darkly threatening. The cuckoo's song, repeating its own name, chimes so closely with "cuckold" that it is a "word of fear, / Unpleasing to a married ear" (V.2.884-85). Spring is, after all, the time for "cuckoo-buds" and also for "lady-smocks" (878-79), which might also punningly remind the audience of the ladies' behavior in the play, mocking the men (ladies' mocks), as well as the way that all cuckolding is a mocking of men, a triumph of a sort by women over their husbands. In a play in which, remarkably, not a single character begins or ends the play married, the cuckoo's threat carries over beyond the play's end to the period after the men's trial for "a twelvemonth and a day," a period that cannot be contained within the compass of a play that covers such a short time span and a trial that neither the audience nor the characters can feel any confidence in their completing successfully. Marriage at the end of *Love's Labor's Lost* is a consummation of courtship and wooing that is not only postponed but also possibly never to be reached. It may be that none of the five men who contemplate their period of ordeal (the King of Navarre and his three lords together with Don Armado, who will "hold the plow for [Jaquenetta's] sweet love three year," 867-68) will ever have to fear the cuckoo's song.

But the assumptions about sexual behavior, particularly female sexual behavior, that underpin the terror of the potential cuckold are spread much more generally through the play. Language in *Love's Labor's Lost* is not only always pregnant with the possibilities of linguistic innovation but also capable of hinting at pregnancy. The chaos that is halted by the arrival of Marcadé, the messenger with the news of the King of France's death, is most immediately provoked by the impending fight between Don Armado and Costard, pale representations as they have been of the great warriors Hector and Pompey, a fight provoked by the announcement that Jaquenetta is two months pregnant by Don Armado: "She is two months on her way" (664). We have only Costard's word for the identity of the father, but it must at least pass through the audience's minds that the father is Costard himself, who was "taken with" Jaquenetta at the play's opening (I.1.198), an event that Don Armado describes as "obscene and most preposterous" (234-35). All the verbs used to describe that encounter between Costard and Jaquenetta – "taken," "sorted and consorted" (248) – have sexual double meanings and, as Costard proudly states, "This maid will serve my turn, sir" (283): Don Armado may be a cuckold before he has even married.

If Jaquenetta's pregnancy can be written off by gentlemen as the natural behavior of a working-class woman, the play's language also resounds with unpleasant gentlemanly assumptions about women of higher class. In part the lords display a humor that we might dub schoolboyish: Berowne's image of his mistress walking along streets "pavèd with thine eyes" immediately provokes Dumaine to think of the street's being able to look up her skirt:

> O vile! Then, as she goes, what upward lies
>   The street should see as she walked overhead.
>   (IV.3.276-77)

But Berowne's long soliloquy of appalled amazement (III.1.170-202) at the discovery that he, the great scorner of Cupid ("A domineering pedant o'er the boy," 174), is himself in love is not, as one might have expected, full of high praise of the woman he has fallen for. Not only is Rosaline "the worst" of the three women, "A whitely wanton with a velvet brow, / With two pitch balls stuck in her face for eyes" (193-94), but he also automatically and unhesitatingly assumes that she is available for sex with anyone and able to evade any watchful controls on her sexual activity:

> Ay, and, by heaven, one that will do the deed,
> Though Argus were her eunuch and her guard.
> And I to sigh for her, to watch for her,
> To pray for her!
>
> (195-98)

Berowne is condemned to perform all the actions of the lover for someone he cannot respect:

> Well, I will love, write, sigh, pray, sue, groan:
> Some men must love my lady, and some Joan.
>
> (201-2)

The last line may be proverbial – "Joan is as good as my lady" – but it often carried an additional phrase, "in the dark," arguing that sex with any woman is equally satisfactory and has nothing to do with rank. If Berowne is infuriated to find himself trapped by Cupid into the ridiculous posturing of the lover, it is not an emotion that can be wholly contained by self-disgust. He seems determined to extend the emotion to an attack on Rosaline, who is viciously condemned for something for which the play never gives any evidence beyond prejudicial male assumptions and female mockery (Katherine identifies Rosaline as "a light wench" – that is, wanton [V.2.25]). Berowne's is an attitude that might affect how we understand his sonnet to Rosaline in the letter that goes astray; its confident claim "I thy parts admire" (IV.2.113) might make an audience wonder which parts in particular Berowne is thinking about, praising her "with such an earthly tongue" (117).

Berowne's all-too-witting earlier comments on Rosaline's determination to have sex are all the more unpleasant given his usual control over language. It is, though, the case that for some in the play, language seems unable to be controlled in its ramifications. There is no reason to suppose that the humble curate Nathaniel has any idea of what is happening when he praises Holofernes the school-teacher: "my parishioners['] . . . daughters profit very greatly under you. You are a good member of the commonwealth" (IV.2.73-75). Perhaps Holofernes has no stronger idea of the implications when his poem in praise of the princess's hunting puns so uncontrollably on "prick" and the letter "l" ("ell"), both of which could refer to a penis.

The nature of *Love's Labor's Lost* that I have been describing is hardly the conventional one. A play usually seen as a witty exchange of courtly wooing seems instead to be barely controlling the sexual desires and sexual attitudes that underpin that wooing. The language of wit seems to veer alarmingly toward a more aggressive taunting over sexual morality and, while the princess lightly sees the exchange between Rosaline and Katherine as a tennis match ("a set of wit well played," V.2.29), the accusatory tone between the two women hints at something fiercely competitive and awkwardly revelatory of their true relationship ("You weigh me not? O, that's you care not for me," line 27).

The men's games of wit tennis with the ladies of France usually see the men comprehensively defeated. If wit is supposed to display mastery, then these lords prove to be inadequately witty, unable to make language show them masters in front of their wished-for mistresses. They are most successful in Berowne's brilliant response to Navarre's desperate plea ("now prove / Our loving lawful and our faith not torn," IV.3.280-81). This time Berowne can make language prove anything, justifying the oath-breaking as a religious necessity:

> Let us once lose our oaths to find ourselves,
> Or else we lose ourselves to keep our oaths.
> It is religion to be thus forsworn.
>
> (335-37)

But if meaning, even of solemn oaths, is so susceptible to reinterpretation, language itself, far from being a site of rigorous control over thought, a means of making ideas work wittily in language, proves to be a dangerously uncontrollable means of communication, manipulable at will and often revealing more than its speaker intends. Language both lays open the speakers' fuller range of meanings than intentional control would be prepared to acknowledge and lays itself open so that its play of potential meanings troubles the patterns of the action. Of course, such a revelation of the practices of language could be found in numerous plays; it is not in itself surprising. But, in connection with a play that has been taken as a revelation of proper aristocratic control over the instabilities of language (something that is embodied in the concept of witty exchanges, the banter and repartee that would lead from *Love's Labor's Lost* eventually to the Restoration comedies of Etherege and Congreve), it offers a play where language careers comically across the interplay between speakers in ways beyond the mastery of discourse that wit is supposed to display.

Holofernes' wit, itself only a pale shadow of the linguistic and rational virtuosity of Berowne, is based on a notion of exactness in language, a clarity of thought to be revealed in forms of pronunciation. His mockery of Don Armado's way with English is a wish that English should be as exactly and completely sounded as is currently the case with, for example, German. The elisions of English speech are unacceptable to Holofernes, the practice of those "rackers of orthography" who pronounce "doubt" without sounding the "b" or "calf" without the "l" (V.1.19-22). But Holofernes' own language is hardly English at all, larded with odd scraps of Latin into a macaronic confusion: "It insinuateth me of *insanire. Ne intelligis, domine?* To make frantic, lunatic" (24-25). But Holofernes seems no saner than the others. It is particularly appropriate that the loudest laughter at a performance of the play is often in response to Dull's explanation of his silence throughout this scene (V.1):

HOLOFERNES   *Via,* goodman Dull! Thou hast spoken no word all this while.
DULL   Nor understood none neither, sir.

(139-41)

In this unnerving world of competing eccentric discourses, the self-centered and maddening languages of Don Armado, Holofernes, Moth, and the others, Dull's silence seems the only sensible response. The scene has come to sound like a kind of Babel.

If, as Moth wisely remarks, "They have been at a great feast of languages and stolen the scraps" (35-36), it must have been a feast with a particularly exotic range of dishes. Each character is – to pursue Moth's metaphor in a way that is characteristic of the play's stretching of an image – what he or she has eaten: it is both that Don Armado enjoys speaking his wonderfully overelaborated language and that the language enjoys creating Don Armado. In a way that makes *Love's Labor's Lost* particularly postmodern, it is difficult to see what Don Armado is other than his unprecedented and inimitable language, one of Shakespeare's greatest achievements in writing comic prose:

Then for the place where – where, I mean, I did encounter that obscene and most preposterous event that draweth from my snow-white pen the ebon-colored ink, which here thou viewest, beholdest, surveyest, or seest.

(I.1.233-37)

It seems natural, in this context, that Moth's height can be measured against the length of a word: "thou art not so long by the head as *honorificabilitudinitatibus*" (V.1.39-40). But the self-centered discourse is characteristic of other languages throughout the play's cast, and almost every character discovers – to his or her cost – that language will not quite do what individuals might wish it to do in their own separate pursuits of a route through the maze of discourses.

The entire action of the play – such as it is, for *Love's Labor's Lost* is hardly a play burdened with an elaborate central plot – is premised on the difficulty of controlling action and meaning through language. The King of Navarre's plan to spend three years studying without the threat of sexual desire being provoked by conversation with a woman anywhere near his academic retreat runs immediately up against the arrival of the Princess of France on matters of state. The plan has been drawn up with great exactness: it excludes any woman, be she wench, damsel, virgin, or maid (I.1.274-83). A clause designed to preserve the would-be scholars from temptation also functions to control the desires of anyone who lives under the king's jurisdiction: Costard is equally constrained by the proclamation based on the solemn oath to which he is not a party. The entire academic project seems in this light more than a little selfish, a reflection of the kind of self-centeredness that has blinkered Navarre to the political implications of his vow.

The project itself was one that Shakespeare's audience might well have associated with France. Pierre de la Primaudaye's fictitious account of a French academy in which four gentlemen from Anjou indulged in endless disputations on political and moral questions had been translated into English in 1586. Hunting and chivalry provide these students with recreation. Shakespeare's Navarre has provided his fellow students with an eccentric, Don Armado, "a refinèd traveler of Spain" (160), though it is difficult to believe that even Don Armado's remarkable way with words will still be amusing after three years. In any case, the king's whole aim, an apparently laudable ambition to devote himself and his friends to scholarship and one enshrined in that solemn oath, cannot possibly be sustained when diplomatic business needs to be dispatched. At the end of his career Shakespeare would return in *The Tempest* to a ruler who scanted state affairs to devote himself to his studies. Prospero's scholarly ambitions resulted in his brother's usurpation and his own exile; Navarre's wish to be absorbed in his studies has an easier resolution. But it involves being forsworn: as Berowne archly points out, the article against conversation with a woman, "my liege, yourself must break" (130).

The king's first response to the difficulty posed by his failing to remember the princess's embassy and its implications for his oath is a refusal to welcome the princess and her attendants to his court, a refusal that causes immediate diplomatic offense:

> KING   Fair princess, welcome to the court of Navarre.
> PRINCESS   "Fair" I give you back again, and "welcome" I have not yet. The roof of this court is too high to be yours, and welcome to the wide fields too base to be mine.
>
> (II.1.90-94)

His later proposal, to "lead you to our court," is not significantly more successful, since his explanation, "The virtue of your eye must break my oath" (V.2.349), is to abuse language: as the princess says, "You nickname virtue. 'Vice' you should have spoke, / For virtue's office never breaks men's troth" (350–51). The oath is unworkable, but it cannot be simply reneged upon without further accusations of offensively illogical and immoral reasoning. The princess's tone here is not that of light wit and wordplay but begins instead to approach a genuine annoyance at the implications of Navarre's behavior.

Whatever becomes the matter of the play for king and princess, lords and ladies, the games of courtliness and courtship that they play, the events can only take place within a defined expanse of time, the period between, on the one hand, the day of her arrival and the following day, when it will be possible to produce the "acquittances" that would prove the King of France's case that the sums have already been paid and force Navarre to hand back Aquitaine and, on the other hand, her return to France. The exact circumstances of these political negotiations over loans and land, debts and repayments, are far from clear in the play, even though elaborately outlined by Navarre (II.1.128-52), and neither Shakespeare nor the audience is much concerned with them.

The link between such diplomatic negotiations and the courtly entertainments in the play may be loosely and distantly related to the events that took place at Nérac in 1578 when Henri of Navarre met with his estranged wife, Marguerite de Valois, and her dangerous mother, Catherine de Médicis, to argue about dowry and see whether there was a chance of reconciliation. The circumstances are hardly especially close to those of *Love's Labor's Lost,* but both a Duc de Longueville and a Duc de Biron were supporters of Navarre, though the Duc de Mayenne (perhaps a source of Shakespeare's Dumaine) was one of Navarre's fiercest opponents. Shakespeare's King of Navarre may be Ferdinand, rather than Henri, but the name is never spoken onstage, appearing only in stage directions and speech prefixes. Since *Love's Labor's Lost* lacks any primary narrative source, no tale from which Shakespeare seems to have derived his plot, the wish to connect the play's action with historical events seems to have been all the stronger a temptation for scholars, but I doubt whether Nérac is more than distantly evoked.

Though the play hardly follows up the narrative over the destiny of Aquitaine, it is clear that the princess has been successful in her embassy, far more so than the parody of ambassadorial activities in the arrival of the lords disguised as a masque of Muscovites, diplomats "to parley, to court and dance" (V.2.122): even at the moment of her rapid departure after the news of her father's death, she takes time to excuse her "coming too short of thanks / For my great suit so easily obtained" (728-29). Even when it comes to crucial state business, it would appear that

Navarre is likely to have made a mistake, and his own elaborate account of the movement of money and obligation proves to have been substantially incorrect.

But the initial delay till the next day, when the arrival of "the packet" is promised, marks out a space for courtship. Since the princess plans to return to France on "Saturday" (IV.1.6), we may assume that the play's events take place on the two preceding days, with the princess arriving on Thursday and the packet arriving on Friday. Shakespeare rarely keeps the time scale of his plays quite as restricted as this. In *The Comedy of Errors,* the single day of the action marks the period within which Egeon must find a ransom or die. In *Love's Labor's Lost* the threat appears less substantial, but the arrival of Marcadé with the tale of death is just as terminal to the play's mood:

MARCADÉ   The king your father –
PRINCESS
  Dead, for my life!
MARCADÉ   Even so. My tale is told.
BEROWNE
  Worthies, away! The scene begins to cloud.
                    (V.2 710-12)

His is a bald statement devoid of wit (the pun on life and death is characteristically the princess's, not his); it is the briefest of tales, one that can be told in only eight words. But it is a tale long enough to make his name come true, for Marcadé's name is another of the play's multiple puns. In sixteenth-century France it was the name for the *danse macabre,* the image of the dance of death. Shakespeare probably found the name in Robert Wilson's *The Cobbler's Prophecy* (written 1588/89, printed 1594), where Ralph the cobbler is visited by Mercury, the gods' messenger, and repeatedly calls him "Markedy." But this messenger's report is enough finally and fatally to *mar* this *arcadia,* the pastoral idyll in which, away from the confines of the indoor spaces of the court, the play's action takes place. With his news it is not only the language but also the expected closure of the play's action that can no longer be contained by the male characters:

KING
    Come, sir, it wants a twelvemonth and a day,
    And then 'twill end.
BEROWNE   That's too long for a play.
                       (V.2.861–62)

Comedy's closure is itself destroyed by the news of death.

The initial description of the King of France as "decrepit, sick, and bed-rid" (I.1.135) is the play's only hint of its crucial late turn, but death has begun to loom more clearly over the last scene. At more than 900 lines, V.2 of *Love's Labor's Lost* is the single longest continuous sequence Shakespeare ever wrote, a massive unfolding scene amounting to well over a third of the whole play; it is as if the whole play thus far has been merely a preparation for what now occurs. Strikingly, it begins and ends with references to death, from Rosaline's mention of Katherine's sister who died for love (13) to Marcadé's report of the King of France's.

In the end it seems particularly fitting that in a play whose characters are so devoted to extravagant excesses of language it should be the entrance of a character, more than anything else, that takes the action in its final direction. Often onstage Marcadé is a magnificent figure, a black-clad courtier entering a world that has been brightly colored. But equally often his entrance can be most effective when barely noticed by the others on the full stage and the audience in the theater. Peter Brook's conception of the play as he worked on it at the Shakespeare Memorial Theatre in Stratford-upon-Avon in 1946 – the production that more than any previous one proved that the

play worked superbly onstage – depended on this moment; as Brook described it,

> It was through this that I brought [Marcadé] over a
> rise at the back of the stage – it was evening, the
> lights were going down, and suddenly there ap-
> peared a man in black. The man in black came onto
> a very pretty summery stage, with everybody in pale
> pastel Watteau and Lancret costumes, and golden
> lights dying. (Peter Brook, *The Shifting Point,* New
> York, 1987, p. 12)

But Brook also recognized that Marcadé's entry is something that always might happen in a Watteau painting:

> Every one of Watteau's paintings has an incredible
> melancholy. And if one looks, one sees that in Wat-
> teau (unlike the imitations of the period, where it's
> all sweetness and prettiness) there is usually a dark
> figure somewhere . . . the dark touch gives the di-
> mension to the whole piece.

Melancholy is intimately associated in *Love's Labor's Lost*
with Don Armado, whose first line asks "what sign is it
when a man of great spirit grows melancholy?" (I.2.1-2).
But by the end, though the king may ask that "at the latest
minute of the hour, / Grant us your loves" (V.2.777-78), a
wish that has a kind of urgency never previously heard in
the play, the women still refuse. As the four French aristocrats unwillingly contemplate their future, it is Don Armado who willingly commits himself to his three years, a
term at once three times as long as the others' and the same
period the men had originally agreed to study. If it is
comic that Armado cannot strip to his shirt for combat
with Costard simply because "I have no shirt" (700), there
is something touching about his penance and his hidden
reminder of the object of his love, wearing "none but a

dishclout of Jaquenetta's, and that a wears next his heart for a favor" (703-4). In his manner of being in love, much more committedly than the others' endless talking of love, Don Armado fittingly speaks the play's last line, its melancholic mark of separations and perhaps of no more meetings:

> The words of Mercury are harsh after the songs of Apollo. You, that way: we, this way.

PETER HOLLAND
The Shakespeare Institute,
The University of Birmingham

Note on the Text

Love's Labor's Lost was published in 1598 in a quarto. The statement on the title page that the text is "Newly corrected and augmented *By W. Shakespere*" suggests that there may have been an earlier printed edition, but no copies of it survive. The copy for Q was probably the lost quarto that had been set from Shakespeare's manuscript. The folio text was probably in part corrected from a playhouse manuscript. The text of Q has a number of errors, especially in the setting of foreign words. Many characters have alternative speech prefixes, so that, for example, Armado also appears as Braggart, the king also as Navarre and Ferdinand, Moth also as Boy and Page, Nathaniel also as Curate, Holofernes also as Pedant, and Dull also as Constable and Anthony. Maria, Katherine, and Rosaline are sometimes identified as Lady, 2 Lady, and 3 Lady. The act and scene division in this edition follows the folio, except in dividing Act I into two scenes. Listed below are all substantive departures from Q, with the Q reading in roman and the adopted reading in italics.

I.1 24 *three* thee   31 *pomp* pome   62 *feast* fast   126–29 *A . . . devise* (part of Longaville's preceding speech in Q; Q gives a s.p. for Berowne at l. 130)   249 *with, with* which with   279 *KING* Ber.
I.2 13–14 *epitheton* apethaton   97 *blushing* blush-in   138 *DULL* (assigned to Costard in Q)   155 *Master* M.
II.1 32 *Importunes* Importuous   34 *visaged* visage   44 *parts* peerelsse   88 *unpeopled* unpeeled   100 *it – will* it will   115–26 *ROSALINE* Kath[erine]   130 *of* of, of   194 *Katherine* Rosalin   195 **s.d.** (not in Q)   209 *Rosaline* Katherin   253–57 (the s.p.'s are based on Q and assume consistency there of Lad., Lad. 2, and Lad. 3 with the uses earlier in the scene – but Shakespeare could well have been inconsistent)
III.1 13 *as if* if   14 *through the* through: 17 *thin-belly* thin-bellies   22–23 *note – do you note? – men that* note: do you note men that   25 *penny* penne   70–71 *the mail* thee male   140, 144, 146, 148, 152,

154, 170, IV.3.279, 285 (Q begins each line with "O," possibly a verbal tic of Berowne's, more probably a misreading of s.p. "Bero." as "Ber. O") 177 *signor-junior* Signior Iunios 187 *clock* Cloake 201 *sue* shue

IV.1 3 *BOYET* Forr. 6 *On* Ore 76 *king's* king 109 *suitor . . . suitor* shooter . . . shooter 131 *hit it* hit 137 *pin is* in 145 *o' th' t' other* 'ath toothen 149 *a most* most

IV.2 29 *we of* we 36 *Dictynna . . . Dictynna* Dictisima . . . dictisima 37 *Dictynna* dictima 51 *call I* cald 53 *scurrility* squirilitie 60 *sores – O sore "l"* sores o sorell: 65–102 (s.p.'s for Nathaniel and Holofernes are reversed in Q) 69 *pia mater* primater 70–71 *in whom* whom 78 *sapit* sapis 95–96 *Venezia . . . perrechia* vemchie, vencha, que non te unde, que non te perreche 104 *NATHANIEL* (not in Q) 118 *apostrophus* apostraphas 119 *canzonet* cangent 119–26 *Here . . . you* (assigned in Q to Nathaniel) 128–33 *I will . . . Browne.* (assigned in Q to Nathaniel) 131 *writing* written 133 *Sir Nathaniel* Sir Holofernes 153 *ben* bien

IV.3 45 *KING* Long 49 *triumviry* triumphery 55 *slop* shop 71 *idolatry* ydotarie 89 *I mine* mine 104 *Wished* wish 108 *thorn* throne 113 *great* (not in Q) 142 *Faith so* Fayth 151 *coaches* couches 176 *like you* like 204 *e'en* and 255 *and usurping* usurping 333 *authors* authour 335 *Let* Lets 357 *Allons! allons* Alone alone

V.1 20 *sine "b"* fine 25 *insanire* infamie 26 *bone* bene 27 *Bone . . . Priscian* Bome boon for boon prescian 30 *gaudeo* gaudio 32 *Quare* Quari 54 *wave* wane 55 *venue* vene we 64 *manu* unum 92 *importunate* importunt 97 *mustachio* mustachie 102 *secrecy* secretie 110 *Sir Nathaniel* Sir Holofernes 112 *rendered* rended; *assistance* assistants 118–19 *Judas . . . Hector* and this gallant Gentleman Iudas Machabeus 142 *Allons* Alone

V.2 17 *been a a* bin 28 *cure . . . care* care . . . cure 43 *ho!* How? 53, 57 *MARIA* Marg. 53 *pearls* Pearle 65 *hests* device 74 *wantonness* wantons be 80 *stabbed* stable 89 *sycamore* siccamone 96 *they* thy 123 *love suit* Love-feat 134 *too* two 148 *her* his 152 *ne'er* ere 159 *BOYET* Berowne 163 *ever* even 217 *The . . . it* (assigned in Q to Rosaline) 243–56 *KATHERINE* Mar[ia] 298 *vailing* varling 310 *run* runnes 408 *affectation* affection 464 *zany* saine 483 *manège* nuage 501 *they* thy 514 *least* best 528 *de la guerra* delaguar 561 *this* his 638 *gilt* gift 663 *The . . . gone* (printed as a s.d. in Q) 680 *on, stir* or stir 768 *the ambassadors* ambassadors 772 *this in our* this our 802 *intitled* intiled 806 *hermit* herrite 808 *A wife* (included in following speech in Q) 876 *Ver, begin* (attributed to "B." in Q) 877 *SPRING* (not in Q) 878, 879 (lines transposed in Q) 899 *foul* full 901, 910 *Tu-who* (omitted in Q) 913–14 *ARMADO . . . omnes* (Q concludes with "The words of Mercury are harsh after the songs of Apollo," printed in larger type below the song. The folio adds the s.p., together with "You, that way: we, this way. Exeunt omnes.", making the words of Q a part of the play.)

Love's Labor's Lost

[NAMES OF THE ACTORS

FERDINAND, *King of Navarre*
BEROWNE ⎫
LONGAVILLE ⎬ *lords attending on the king*
DUMAINE ⎭
DON ADRIANO DE ARMADO, *a Spanish braggart*
MOTH, *his page*
PRINCESS OF FRANCE
ROSALINE ⎫
KATHERINE ⎬ *ladies attending on the princess*
MARIA ⎭
BOYET ⎫
TWO LORDS ⎬ *attending on the princess*
COSTARD, *a clown*
JAQUENETTA, *a dairymaid*
SIR NATHANIEL, *a curate*
HOLOFERNES, *a schoolteacher*
ANTHONY DULL, *a constable*
MARCADÉ, *a messenger*
A FORESTER
MUSICIANS

SCENE: *Navarre*]
*

Love's Labor's Lost

∿ **I.1** *Enter Ferdinand King of Navarre, Berowne,*
Longaville, and Dumaine.

KING
> Let fame, that all hunt after in their lives,
> Live registered upon our brazen tombs   2
> And then grace us in the disgrace of death,   3
> When, spite of cormorant devouring Time,   4
> Th' endeavor of this present breath may buy   5
> That honor which shall bate his scythe's keen edge   6
> And make us heirs of all eternity.
> Therefore, brave conquerors – for so you are
> That war against your own affections   9
> And the huge army of the world's desires –   10
> Our late edict shall strongly stand in force: 11
> Navarre shall be the wonder of the world;
> Our court shall be a little academe,   13
> Still and contemplative in living art.   14

I.1 The action throughout the play takes place in the King of Navarre's park.
s.d. *Ferdinand* (the name "Ferdinand" is never spoken in the play and appears only in stage directions and speech prefixes in I.1 and II.1; it was probably Shakespeare's first thought); *Berowne* (a transliteration of "Biron," probably pronounced "b'roon" – it rhymes with "moon" at IV.3.226); *Longaville* (the last syllable is rhymed with "ill," IV.3.120, "compile," IV.3.130, and puns with "veal" at V.2.248); *Dumaine* (a transliteration of Duc de Mayenne) **2** *brazen* brass (i.e., enduring) **3** *grace* honor; *disgrace of death* (1) the loss of the grace of life by dying, (2) the shaming of death (by fame), (3) the disfigurement death will cause us **4** *cormorant* ravenous (like the seabird) **5** *breath* breathing-time (i.e., life), speech **6** *bate* blunt **9** *affections* passions **11** *late* recent **13** *academe* academy **14** *Still* constant, calm; *living art* (1) art of living, (2) making learning (art) invigorated by life

You three – Berowne, Dumaine, and Longaville –
Have sworn for three years' term to live with me
My fellow scholars, and to keep those statutes
18   That are recorded in this schedule here.
19   Your oaths are passed; and now subscribe your names,
20   That his own hand may strike his honor down
21   That violates the smallest branch herein.
22   If you are armed to do as sworn to do,
Subscribe to your deep oaths, and keep it too.

LONGAVILLE
I am resolved. 'Tis but a three years' fast.
The mind shall banquet though the body pine.
26   Fat paunches have lean pates, and dainty bits
Make rich the ribs, but bankrupt quite the wits.

DUMAINE
28   My loving lord, Dumaine is mortified.
The grosser manner of these world's delights
30   He throws upon the gross world's baser slaves.
To love, to wealth, to pomp, I pine and die,
32   With all these living in philosophy.

BEROWNE
33   I can but say their protestation over.
34   So much, dear liege, I have already sworn,
That is, to live and study here three years.
But there are other strict observances:
As not to see a woman in that term,
38   Which I hope well is not enrollèd there;
And one day in a week to touch no food,
40   And but one meal on every day beside,
The which I hope is not enrollèd there;
And then to sleep but three hours in the night,

---

18 *schedule* document   19 *passed* pledged   20 *hand* handwriting (also "armed hand")   21 *branch* clause   22 *armed* prepared   26 *pates* heads; *dainty bits* delicate morsels   28 *mortified* i.e., dead to desire   32 *all these* (1) his companions, (2) love, wealth, pomp, for which philosophy will prove the substitute, (3) the conditions in the "schedule"   33 *over* again   34 *liege* sovereign   38 *well* fervently

And not be seen to wink of all the day   43
(When I was wont to think no harm all night   44
And make a dark night too of half the day),
Which I hope well is not enrollèd there.
O, these are barren tasks, too hard to keep –
Not to see ladies, study, fast, not sleep.

KING
Your oath is passed to pass away from these.

BEROWNE
Let me say no, my liege, an if you please.   50
I only swore to study with your grace
And stay here in your court for three years' space.

LONGAVILLE
You swore to that, Berowne, and to the rest.

BEROWNE
By yea and nay, sir, then I swore in jest.   54
What is the end of study, let me know?

KING
Why, that to know which else we should not know.

BEROWNE
Things hid and barred, you mean, from common sense?   57

KING
Ay, that is study's godlike recompense.

BEROWNE
Come on then, I will swear to study so,   59
To know the thing I am forbid to know,   60
As thus – to study where I well may dine
    When I to feast expressly am forbid;
Or study where to meet some mistress fine
    When mistresses from common sense are hid;
Or having sworn too hard-a-keeping oath,
Study to break it and not break my troth.

---

43 *wink* close the eyes, nap   44 *wont* accustomed; *think no harm* think it no
harm to sleep   50 *an if* if   54 *By . . . nay* (1) irrevocably (derived in popular
usage from Matthew 5:37), (2) equivocally (in Berowne's play on the literal
meaning)   57 *common sense* ordinary observation   59 *Come on* (punning on
"common," l. 57)

If study's gain be thus, and this be so,
68 Study knows that which yet it doth not know.
Swear me to this, and I will ne'er say no.

KING
70 These be the stops that hinder study quite,
71 And train our intellects to vain delight.

BEROWNE
72 Why, all delights are vain, but that most vain
73 Which, with pain purchased, doth inherit pain:
As, painfully to pore upon a book,
To seek the light of truth, while truth the while
76 Doth falsely blind the eyesight of his look.
77 Light seeking light doth light of light beguile;
So, ere you find where light in darkness lies,
79 Your light grows dark by losing of your eyes.
80 Study me how to please the eye indeed,
81 By fixing it upon a fairer eye,
82 Who dazzling so, that eye shall be his heed,
83 And give him light that it was blinded by.
Study is like the heaven's glorious sun,
85 That will not be deep-searched with saucy looks:
Small have continual plodders ever won,
Save base authority from others' books.
88 These earthly godfathers of heaven's lights,
That give a name to every fixèd star,
90 Have no more profit of their shining nights
91 Than those that walk and wot not what they are.
92 Too much to know is to know nought but fame;
93 And every godfather can give a name.

---

68 study here knows the kind of thing (i.e., hidden knowledge) that, up to now, it has not   70 stops impediments   71 train allure   72 vain foolish, proud   73 purchased acquired; inherit take possession of   76 falsely treacherously; his look its power to see   77 i.e., peering for truth deprives the eyes of their sight   79 light sight   80–93 (a sonnet)   80 Study me study, I say   81 a fairer eye the eye of a fair woman   82 dazzling so thus bedazzled; heed guide   83 it i.e., his eye   85 saucy insolent   88 earthly godfathers i.e., the astronomers   90 shining i.e., star-lit   91 wot know   92 know nought experience nothing; fame hearsay   93 every . . . name i.e., anyone who serves as a godfather can do as much as astronomers do

KING
How well he's read to reason against reading!   94
DUMAINE
Proceeded well, to stop all good proceeding!   95
LONGAVILLE
He weeds the corn, and still lets grow the weeding.   96
BEROWNE
The spring is near, when green geese are a-breeding.   97
DUMAINE
How follows that?   98
BEROWNE   Fit in his place and time.
DUMAINE
In reason nothing.   99
BEROWNE   Something then in rhyme.
KING
Berowne is like an envious sneaping frost   100
That bites the first-born infants of the spring.   101
BEROWNE
Well, say I am; why should proud summer boast   102
Before the birds have any cause to sing?
Why should I joy in any abortive birth?
At Christmas I no more desire a rose
Than wish a snow in May's newfangled shows,
But like of each thing that in season grows.   107
So you, to study now it is too late,   108
Climb o'er the house to unlock the little gate.   109
KING
Well, sit you out. Go home, Berowne. Adieu.   *110*
BEROWNE
No, my good lord, I have sworn to stay with you;

---

94 *read . . . reading* studied . . . studying   95 *Proceeded* argued; *proceeding*
taking an academic degree   96 *weeds the corn* i.e., pulls up the wheat; *weed-*
ing weeds   97 *green geese* young geese, fools   98 *Fit in his* precisely in its
99 it is not logical but it does rhyme   100 *sneaping* nipping   101 *first-born*
infants i.e., early buds   102–3 *why . . . sing* i.e., why should summer appear
unseasonably   107 *like of* enjoy   108 *too late* i.e., past his student days
109 *Climb . . . gate* i.e., act perversely (proverbial)

112 And though I have for barbarism spoke more
        Than for that angel knowledge you can say,
     Yet confident I'll keep what I have sworn,
115   And bide the penance of each three years' day.
     Give me the paper, let me read the same,
     And to the strict'st decrees I'll write my name.
KING   *[Handing over the paper]*
     How well this yielding rescues thee from shame!
BEROWNE   *[Reads.]* "Item: that no woman shall come
120 within a mile of my court –" Hath this been proclaimed?
LONGAVILLE   Four days ago.
BEROWNE   Let's see the penalty. "– on pain of losing her
     tongue." Who devised this penalty?
LONGAVILLE
124 Marry, that did I.
BEROWNE   Sweet lord, and why?
LONGAVILLE
     To fright them hence with that dread penalty.
BEROWNE
126 A dangerous law against gentility!
        [Reads.]
     "Item: if any man be seen to talk with a woman within
     the term of three years, he shall endure such public
     shame as the rest of the court can possible devise."
130 This article, my liege, yourself must break;
        For well you know here comes in embassy
     The French king's daughter with yourself to speak,
        A maid of grace and complete majesty,
134 About surrender up of Aquitaine
        To her decrepit, sick, and bed-rid father.
     Therefore this article is made in vain,
        Or vainly comes th' admirèd princess hither.
KING
     What say you, lords? why, this was quite forgot.

---

112 *for barbarism* on behalf of ignorance   115 *bide . . . day* i.e., endure the
deprivation of each day of the three years   124 *Marry* by Mary (mild oath)
126 *gentility* good manners   134 *Aquitaine* a district of southwest France

BEROWNE

 So study evermore is overshot.

 While it doth study to have what it would,   *140*

 It doth forget to do the thing it should,

 And when it hath the thing it hunteth most,

 'Tis won as towns with fire – so won, so lost.   143

KING

 We must of force dispense with this decree;   144

 She must lie here on mere necessity.   145

BEROWNE

 Necessity will make us all forsworn

  Three thousand times within this three years' space:

 For every man with his affects is born,   148

  Not by might mastered, but by special grace.   149

 If I break faith, this word shall speak for me: 150

 I am forsworn "on mere necessity."

 So to the laws at large I write my name;

  [Signs.]

 And he that breaks them in the least degree

 Stands in attainder of eternal shame.   154

 Suggestions are to other as to me;   155

 But I believe, although I seem so loath,

 I am the last that will last keep his oath.   157

 But is there no quick recreation granted?   158

KING

 Ay, that there is. Our court you know is haunted   159

  With a refinèd traveler of Spain,   *160*

 A man in all the world's new fashion planted,   161

  That hath a mint of phrases in his brain;

 One who the music of his own vain tongue   163

  Doth ravish like enchanting harmony;

---

143 *as . . . fire* i.e., like towns conquered by being burned down **144** *of force* perforce **145** *lie* lodge; *on mere* out of absolute **148** *affects* passions **149** *might* i.e., his own strength; *special grace* heavenly intervention **150** *word* phrase **154** *in attainder* under penalty **155** *Suggestions* temptations **157** (1) I signed last but will keep my oath longest, (2) I am the least likely to keep my oath longest **158** *quick* lively **159–60** *haunted / With* frequented by **161** *planted* rooted **163** *who* whom

165 A man of complements, whom right and wrong
166   Have chose as umpire of their mutiny.
167 This child of fancy, that Armado hight,
168   For interim to our studies shall relate
169 In high-born words the worth of many a knight
170   From tawny Spain, lost in the world's debate.
How you delight, my lords, I know not, I;
But, I protest, I love to hear him lie,
173 And I will use him for my minstrelsy.

BEROWNE
Armado is a most illustrious wight,
175 A man of fire-new words, fashion's own knight.

LONGAVILLE
176 Costard the swain and he shall be our sport,
And so to study three years is but short.
    Enter [Dull,] a Constable with a letter, with Costard.

178 DULL   Which is the duke's own person?
BEROWNE   This, fellow. What wouldst?
180 DULL   I myself reprehend his own person, for I am his
181 grace's farborough; but I would see his own person in flesh and blood.
BEROWNE   This is he.
184 DULL   Señor Arm – Arm – commends you. There's villainy abroad. This letter will tell you more.
186 COSTARD   Sir, the contempts thereof are as touching me.
187 KING   A letter from the magnificent Armado.
BEROWNE   How low soever the matter, I hope in God for high words.

---

165 *complements* accomplishments, formal manners 166 *mutiny* discord 167 *child of fancy* fantastic creature; *hight* is called 168 *interim* interlude 169 *high-born* i.e., highfalutin 170 *tawny* sunburned; *debate* warfare 173 *minstrelsy* i.e., diversion 175 *fire-new* brand-new 176 *Costard* (1) a variety of large apples, (2) slang for "head"; *swain* country youth 178 *duke's* (Is the error – for "king's" – Dull's or Shakespeare's? Also at I.2.36 and 121.) 180 *reprehend* (for "represent") 181 *farborough* petty constable (for "thirdborough") 184 *commends* greets 186 *contempts* (for "contents") 187 *magnificent Armado* (punning on the "Great Armada," the Spanish invasion fleet of 1588)

LONGAVILLE   A high hope for a low heaven. God grant us   190
patience!

BEROWNE   To hear, or forbear hearing?   192

LONGAVILLE   To hear meekly, sir, and to laugh moder-
ately, or to forbear both.

BEROWNE   Well, sir, be it as the style shall give us cause to   195
climb in the merriness.

COSTARD   The matter is to me, sir, as concerning Jaque-   197
netta. The manner of it is, I was taken with the manner.   198

BEROWNE   In what manner?

COSTARD   In manner and form following, sir; all those   200
three: I was seen with her in the manor house, sitting
with her upon the form, and taken following her into   202
the park; which, put together, is "in manner and form
following." Now, sir, for the manner: it is the manner
of a man to speak to a woman. For the form: in some
form.

BEROWNE   For the following, sir?

COSTARD   As it shall follow in my correction, and God   208
defend the right!

KING   Will you hear this letter with attention?   210

BEROWNE   As we would hear an oracle.

COSTARD   Such is the simplicity of man to hearken after   212
the flesh.

KING   *[Reads.]* "Great deputy, the welkin's vicegerent,   214
and sole dominator of Navarre, my soul's earth's God,
and body's fostering patron —"

COSTARD   Not a word of Costard yet.

KING   "So it is —"

---

190 *low heaven* i.e., small blessing   192 *To hear . . . hearing* i.e., to take it or
leave it (editors often emend "hearing" to "laughing")   195 *be it* so be it;
style (punning on "stile," hence "climb")   197 *is to* applies to   198 *with the
manner* in the act (from the legal term "mainour")   202 *form* bench   208
correction punishment   208–9 *God . . . right* (prayer before trial by combat;
Costard is offering to fight Armado)   212 *simplicity* folly (Q's "sinplicitie"
may be a joke)   214 *welkin's vicegerent* heaven's deputy

COSTARD   It may be so; but if he say it is so, he is, in
220   telling true, but so.
KING   Peace!
COSTARD   Be to me and every man that dares not fight.
KING   No words!
COSTARD   Of other men's secrets, I beseech you.
225   KING   "So it is, besieged with sable-colored melancholy, I
226   did commend the black-oppressing humor to the most
227   wholesome physic of thy health-giving air; and, as I am
a gentleman, betook myself to walk. The time when?
About the sixth hour, when beasts most graze, birds
230   best peck, and men sit down to that nourishment
which is called supper: so much for the time when.
Now for the ground which – which, I mean, I walked
233   upon: it is ycleped thy park. Then for the place where –
where, I mean, I did encounter that obscene and most
235   preposterous event that draweth from my snow-white
236   pen the ebon-colored ink, which here thou viewest, beholdest, surveyest, or seest. But to the place where; it
standeth north-northeast and by east from the west cor-
239   ner of thy curious-knotted garden. There did I see that
240   low-spirited swain, that base minnow of thy mirth –"
COSTARD   Me?
KING   "that unlettered small-knowing soul –"
COSTARD   Me?
244   KING   "that shallow vassal –"
COSTARD   Still me.
246   KING   "which, as I remember, hight Costard –"
COSTARD   O me!
248   KING   "sorted and consorted, contrary to thy established
249   proclaimed edict and continent canon, with, with, O
250   with – but with this I passion to say wherewith –"

---

220 *but so* only so-so   225 *sable-colored* black   226 *humor* mood   227
physic medicine   233 *ycleped* called   235–36 *snow-white pen* white quill
236 *ebon-colored* black (like ebony)   239 *curious-knotted* intricately pat-
terned   240 *minnow* i.e., small-fry   244 *vassal* (punning on "vessel")   246
hight is called   248 *sorted* associated   249 *continent canon* law enjoining
celibacy   250 *passion* grieve

COSTARD   With a wench.

KING   "with a child of our grandmother Eve, a female, or, for thy more sweet understanding, a woman. Him I (as my ever-esteemed duty pricks me on) have sent to 254 thee, to receive the meed of punishment, by thy sweet 255 grace's officer, Anthony Dull, a man of good repute, carriage, bearing, and estimation."

DULL   Me, an't shall please you, I am Anthony Dull.

KING   "For Jaquenetta (so is the weaker vessel called), which I apprehended with the aforesaid swain, I keep 260 her as a vessel of thy law's fury; and shall, at the least of 261 thy sweet notice, bring her to trial. Thine in all compli- 262 ments of devoted and heart-burning heat of duty,
                    Don Adriano de Armado."

BEROWNE   This is not so well as I looked for, but the best that ever I heard.

KING   Ay, the best for the worst. But, sirrah, what say 267 you to this?

COSTARD   Sir, I confess the wench.

KING   Did you hear the proclamation? 270

COSTARD   I do confess much of the hearing it, but little of the marking of it. 272

KING   It was proclaimed a year's imprisonment to be taken with a wench.

COSTARD   I was taken with none, sir, I was taken with a damsel.

KING   Well, it was proclaimed "damsel."

COSTARD   This was no damsel neither, sir, she was a virgin.

KING   It is so varied too, for it was proclaimed "virgin." 279

COSTARD   If it were, I deny her virginity. I was taken 280 with a maid.

KING   This maid will not serve your turn, sir. 282

---

254 *pricks* spurs   255 *meed* reward   261–62 *at . . . notice* i.e., at your first hint   262 *to trial* (perhaps punning on "have sex with")   267 *best . . . worst* i.e., prize example of the bad; *sirrah* (term of address to inferiors)   272 *marking of* paying attention to   279 *varied* (the proclamation used strings of synonyms in the style of most legal documents)   282 *turn* purpose (Costard puns on "suitable to have sex with")

COSTARD   This maid will serve my turn, sir.

KING   Sir, I will pronounce your sentence: you shall fast a week with bran and water.

286   COSTARD   I had rather pray a month with mutton and porridge.

KING

And Don Armado shall be your keeper.

My Lord Berowne, see him delivered o'er,

290   And go we, lords, to put in practice that

Which each to other hath so strongly sworn.

[Exeunt King, Longaville, and Dumaine.]

BEROWNE

I'll lay my head to any good man's hat,

These oaths and laws will prove an idle scorn.

Sirrah, come on.

COSTARD   I suffer for the truth, sir; for true it is I was taken with Jaquenetta, and Jaquenetta is a true girl, and

297   therefore welcome the sour cup of prosperity! Affliction

298   may one day smile again, and till then sit thee down, sorrow!   *Exeunt.*

*

∿ **I.2** *Enter Armado, [a Braggart,] and Moth, his Page.*

ARMADO   Boy, what sign is it when a man of great spirit grows melancholy?

MOTH   A great sign, sir, that he will look sad.

ARMADO   Why, sadness is one and the selfsame thing,

5   dear imp.

MOTH   No, no. O Lord, sir, no!

286–87 *mutton and porridge* mutton broth (punning on "mutton," meaning "prostitute")   **297** *prosperity! Affliction* (Costard gets them back to front) **298** *sit thee down* i.e., abide with me

    I.2 s.d. *Moth* (some editors emend to "Mote," "speck of dust," but Costard calls him a "nit" [="insect"] at IV.1.149; "moth" and "mote" were pronounced the same, "mott")   **5** *imp* child

ARMADO   How canst thou part sadness and melancholy,   7
   my tender juvenal?   8
MOTH   By a familiar demonstration of the working, my 9
   tough señor.   10
ARMADO   Why tough señor? why tough señor?
MOTH   Why tender juvenal? why tender juvenal?
ARMADO   I spoke it, tender juvenal, as a congruent epi-   13
   theton appertaining to thy young days, which we may
   nominate "tender."
MOTH   And I, tough señor, as an appertinent title to   16
   your old time, which we may name "tough."
ARMADO   Pretty, and apt.
MOTH   How mean you, sir? I pretty, and my saying apt?
   or I apt, and my saying pretty?   20
ARMADO   Thou pretty, because little.
MOTH   Little pretty, because little. Wherefore apt?
ARMADO   And therefore apt, because quick.   23
MOTH   Speak you this in my praise, master?
ARMADO   In thy condign praise.   25
MOTH   I will praise an eel with the same praise.
ARMADO   What, that an eel is ingenious?
MOTH   That an eel is quick.
ARMADO   I do say thou art quick in answers. Thou
   heat'st my blood.   30
MOTH   I am answered, sir.
ARMADO   I love not to be crossed.
MOTH   [Aside] He speaks the mere contrary – crosses   33
   love not him.
ARMADO   I have promised to study three years with the
   duke.   36
MOTH   You may do it in an hour, sir.

---

7 *part* distinguish between   8 *juvenal* (punning on the Roman satirist "Juvenal" and "juvenile")   9 *working* operation   10 *señor* sir (with pun on "senior")   13–14 *congruent epitheton* appropriate epithet   16 *appertinent*
belonging   23 *quick* quick-witted   25 *condign* well-merited   30 *heat'st my
blood* anger me   33 *crosses* coins (which were commonly stamped with
crosses)   36 *duke* i.e., the ruler, actually a king

ARMADO   Impossible.

MOTH   How many is one thrice told?

40 ARMADO   I am ill at reckoning; it fitteth the spirit of a
41   tapster.

42 MOTH   You are a gentleman and a gamester, sir.

43 ARMADO   I confess both. They are both the varnish of a
  complete man.

MOTH   Then, I am sure you know how much the gross
46   sum of deuce-ace amounts to.

ARMADO   It doth amount to one more than two.

48 MOTH   Which the base vulgar do call three.

ARMADO   True.

50 MOTH   Why, sir, is this such a piece of study? Now here
  is three studied ere ye'll thrice wink; and how easy it is
  to put "years" to the word "three," and study three years
53   in two words, the dancing horse will tell you.

54 ARMADO   A most fine figure.

55 MOTH   *[Aside]* To prove you a cipher.

ARMADO   I will hereupon confess I am in love; and as it
  is base for a soldier to love, so am I in love with a base
58   wench. If drawing my sword against the humor of affection would deliver me from the reprobate thought of
60   it, I would take Desire prisoner and ransom him to any
61   French courtier for a new-devised curtsy. I think scorn
62   to sigh: methinks I should outswear Cupid. Comfort
  me, boy. What great men have been in love?

MOTH   Hercules, master.

ARMADO   Most sweet Hercules! More authority, dear
  boy, name more; and, sweet my child, let them be men
67   of good repute and carriage.

---

40 *I am . . . reckoning* I can't do sums   **41** *tapster* bartender   **42** *gamester* gambler   **43** *varnish* ornament, finish   **46** *deuce-ace* a two and a one in playing dice   **48** *vulgar* common people   **53** *dancing horse* (a performing horse, trained to "count" in hoofbeats; the most famous of the time was Master Banks's horse Morocco)   **54** *figure* rhetorical flourish   **55** *cipher* zero (with play on "numeral")   **58–59** *humor of affection* inclination to passion   **61** *new-devised curtsy* i.e., newfangled French bow (abundant and worthless); *think scorn* disdain   **62** *outswear* forswear   **67** *carriage* bearing

MOTH   Samson, master – he was a man of good carriage,
great carriage, for he carried the town gates on his back   69
like a porter, and he was in love.   70

ARMADO   O well-knit Samson! strong-jointed Samson! I
do excel thee in my rapier as much as thou didst me in
carrying gates. I am in love too. Who was Samson's
love, my dear Moth?

MOTH   A woman, master.

ARMADO   Of what complexion?   76

MOTH   Of all the four, or the three, or the two, or one of   77
the four.

ARMADO   Tell me precisely of what complexion.

MOTH   Of the sea-water green, sir.   80

ARMADO   Is that one of the four complexions?

MOTH   As I have read, sir, and the best of them too.

ARMADO   Green indeed is the color of lovers; but to have   83
a love of that color, methinks Samson had small reason
for it. He surely affected her for her wit.   85

MOTH   It was so, sir, for she had a green wit.   86

ARMADO   My love is most immaculate white and red.

MOTH   Most maculate thoughts, master, are masked   88
under such colors.

ARMADO   Define, define, well-educated infant.   90

MOTH   My father's wit, and my mother's tongue, assist
me!

ARMADO   Sweet invocation of a child, most pretty and
pathetical.   94

---

69 *carried . . . back* (cf. Judges 16:3)   **76** *complexion* (1) skin coloring, (2) disposition (deriving from the balance or imbalance of the four bodily "humors" – blood, choler, phlegm, melancholy)   **77–78** *Of . . . four* (probably an allusion to woman's changeableness)   **80** (chlorosis, an anemic condition that affected young women)   **83** *Green . . . lovers* i.e., lovers are prone to "greensickness" (the melancholy of frustration)   **83–84** *have a love of* i.e., love   **85** *affected . . . wit* liked for her intelligence   **86** *green wit* (1) immature mind, (2) a play on the "green withes" with which Delilah bound Samson (cf. Judges 16:7–9)   **88** *maculate* impure   **94** *pathetical* moving

MOTH

95

> If she be made of white and red,
>   Her faults will ne'er be known,
> For blushing cheeks by faults are bred,
>   And fears by pale white shown;
> Then if she fear, or be to blame,

100

>   By this you shall not know,
> For still her cheeks possess the same

102

>   Which native she doth owe.

103 A dangerous rhyme, master, against the reason of white and red.

105 ARMADO Is there not a ballad, boy, of the King and the Beggar?

MOTH The world was very guilty of such a ballad some three ages since; but I think now 'tis not to be found, or

109
110 if it were, it would neither serve for the writing nor the tune.

ARMADO I will have that subject newly writ o'er, that I

112 may example my digression by some mighty precedent. Boy, I do love that country girl that I took in the park

114 with the rational hind Costard. She deserves well.

115 MOTH *[Aside]* To be whipped – and yet a better love than my master.

ARMADO Sing, boy. My spirit grows heavy in love.

118 MOTH And that's great marvel, loving a light wench.

ARMADO I say, sing.

120 MOTH Forbear till this company be past.

Enter [Costard the] Clown, Constable [Dull], and [Jaquenetta, a] Wench.

---

95 *made* (punning on "maid")   **102** *native* naturally, by birth; *owe* own   **103** *the reason of* the case for   **105–6** *King . . . Beggar* (the ballad of King Cophetua, who fell in love with a beggar maid; cf. IV.1.67–68)   **109** *serve* be accepted (because old-fashioned)   **112** *example* justify; *digression* deviation, lapse   **114** *rational* i.e., rational for a yokel (patronizing rather than complimentary); *hind* rustic   **115** *whipped* (as a prostitute); *love* partner in a love affair   **118** *light* wanton

DULL   Sir, the duke's pleasure is that you keep Costard
safe, and you must suffer him to take no delight nor no
penance, but a must fast three days a week. For this   123
damsel, I must keep her at the park; she is allowed for   124
the deywoman. Fare you well.

ARMADO   I do betray myself with blushing. Maid!

JAQUENETTA   Man!

ARMADO   I will visit thee at the lodge.

JAQUENETTA   That's hereby.

ARMADO   I know where it is situate.   130

JAQUENETTA   Lord, how wise you are!

ARMADO   I will tell thee wonders.

JAQUENETTA   With that face?   133

ARMADO   I love thee.

JAQUENETTA   So I heard you say.

ARMADO   And so farewell.

JAQUENETTA   Fair weather after you!

DULL   Come, Jaquenetta, away!

                    Exeunt [Dull and Jaquenetta].

ARMADO   Villain, thou shalt fast for thy offenses ere thou   139
be pardoned.   140

COSTARD   Well, sir, I hope when I do it I shall do it on a   141
full stomach.

ARMADO   Thou shalt be heavily punished.

COSTARD   I am more bound to you than your fellows,
for they are but lightly rewarded.

ARMADO   Take away this villain. Shut him up.

MOTH   Come, you transgressing slave, away!

COSTARD   Let me not be pent up, sir. I will fast, being   148
loose.

MOTH   No, sir; that were fast and loose. Thou shalt to   150
prison.

---

123 *penance* (an error, possibly for "pleasaunce"); *a* he   124–25 *allowed . . .
deywoman* approved as the dairymaid   133 *With that face* i.e., you don't say
so (slang)   139 *Villain* peasant, rascal   141–42 *on . . . stomach* (1) coura-
geously, (2) well fed   148 *pent up* (1) imprisoned, (2) constipated   148–49
being loose (1) free, (2) having loose bowels   150 *fast and loose* cheating (deriving from a game involving cheating and associated with gypsies)

152 COSTARD   Well, if ever I do see the merry days of desolation that I have seen, some shall see –
MOTH   What shall some see?
COSTARD   Nay, nothing, Master Moth, but what they
look upon. It is not for prisoners to be too silent in
their words, and therefore I will say nothing. I thank
God I have as little patience as another man, and therefore I can be quiet.   *Exit [with Moth]*.
160 ARMADO   I do affect the very ground (which is base)
where her shoe (which is baser) guided by her foot
(which is basest) doth tread. I shall be forsworn (which
163 is a great argument of falsehood) if I love. And how can
that be true love which is falsely attempted? Love is a
165 familiar. Love is a devil. There is no evil angel but Love.
Yet was Samson so tempted, and he had an excellent
strength; yet was Solomon so seduced, and he had
168 a very good wit. Cupid's butt shaft is too hard for
Hercules' club, and therefore too much odds for a
170 Spaniard's rapier. The first and second cause will not
171 serve my turn: the passado he respects not, the duello
he regards not. His disgrace is to be called boy, but his
glory is to subdue men. Adieu, valor! rust, rapier! be
174 still, drum! for your manager is in love; yea, he loveth.
175 Assist me some extemporal god of rhyme, for I am sure
176 I shall turn sonnet. Devise, wit! write, pen! for I am for
177 whole volumes in folio.   *Exit*.

                              *

152–53 *desolation* (malapropism for "consolation")   160 *affect* love   163
argument proof   165 *familiar* evil spirit   168 *butt shaft* unbarbed target
arrow   170 *first . . . cause* (an allusion to certain procedures dictated by the
punctilio of the dueling code)   171 *passado* fencing thrust; *duello* dueling
code   174 *manager* skilled manipulator   175 *extemporal . . . rhyme* god of
fluent occasional verses   176 *turn sonnet* compose a sonnet, turn sonneteer
177 *folio* (largest size of book)

∾ **II.1** *Enter the Princess of France, with three attending Ladies, [Rosaline, Maria, Katherine,] and three Lords [, one of whom is Boyet].*

BOYET
Now, madam, summon up your dearest spirits.   1
Consider who the king your father sends,
To whom he sends, and what's his embassy: 3
Yourself, held precious in the world's esteem,
To parley with the sole inheritor   5
Of all perfections that a man may owe,   6
Matchless Navarre; the plea of no less weight   7
Than Aquitaine, a dowry for a queen.
Be now as prodigal of all dear grace
As Nature was in making graces dear,   10
When she did starve the general world beside,   11
And prodigally gave them all to you.   12
PRINCESS
Good Lord Boyet, my beauty, though but mean,
Needs not the painted flourish of your praise: 14
Beauty is bought by judgment of the eye,
Not uttered by base sale of chapmen's tongues.   16
I am less proud to hear you tell my worth   17
Than you much willing to be counted wise
In spending your wit in the praise of mine.
But now to task the tasker; good Boyet,   20
You are not ignorant all-telling fame
Doth noise abroad Navarre hath made a vow
Till painful study shall outwear three years,   23
No woman may approach his silent court.
Therefore to's seemeth it a needful course,   25

II.1 s.d. *Boyet* (pronounced "boy yet")   1 *dearest spirits* best wits   3 *what's* the nature of   5 *inheritor* possessor   6 *owe* own   7 *plea* suit   11 *beside* except you   12 *prodigally* extravagantly, generously   14 *flourish* adornment   16 *uttered* vended; *chapmen's* retailers'   17 *tell* speak of (with play on "count")   20 *task* assign tasks to   23 *painful* strenuous; *outwear* last out   25 *to's* to us (royal plural)

Before we enter his forbidden gates,
To know his pleasure; and in that behalf,
28   Bold of your worthiness, we single you
29   As our best-moving fair solicitor.
30   Tell him, the daughter of the King of France,
On serious business, craving quick dispatch,
Importunes personal conference with his grace.
Haste, signify so much, while we attend,
Like humble-visaged suitors, his high will.

BOYET
35   Proud of employment, willingly I go.

PRINCESS
36   All pride is willing pride, and yours is so.   *Exit Boyet.*
37   Who are the votaries, my loving lords,
That are vow fellows with this virtuous duke?

LORD
Longaville is one.

PRINCESS   Know you the man?

MARIA
40   I know him, madam. At a marriage feast
41   Between Lord Périgord and the beauteous heir
Of Jaques Fauconbridge solemnizèd
In Normandy saw I this Longaville.
A man of sovereign parts he is esteemed,
45   Well fitted in arts, glorious in arms;
46   Nothing becomes him ill that he would well.
47   The only soil of his fair virtue's gloss
(If virtue's gloss will stain with any soil)
49   Is a sharp wit matched with too blunt a will,
50   Whose edge hath power to cut, whose will still wills

---

28 *Bold* confident   29 *best-moving fair* most persuasive and just   35 *Proud of* honored with   36 *All . . . pride* i.e., all pride derives from man's will   37 *votaries* those living under a vow, often including a vow of celibacy   41, 42 *Lord Périgord, Jaques Fauconbridge* (fictitious persons)   45 *fitted in arts* equipped with learning   46 *Nothing . . . well* i.e., lacking in no grace he values   47 *soil of* blot on   49 *blunt* ruthless   50 *Whose edge* i.e., the edge of his sharp wit

It should none spare that come within his power.
PRINCESS
Some merry mocking lord, belike – is't so?
MARIA
They say so most that most his humors know.
PRINCESS
Such short-lived wits do wither as they grow.
Who are the rest?
KATHERINE
The young Dumaine, a well-accomplished youth,
Of all that virtue love for virtue loved;   57
Most power to do most harm, least knowing ill,   58
For he hath wit to make an ill shape good,   59
And shape to win grace though he had no wit.   60
I saw him at the Duke Alençon's once;
And much too little of that good I saw   62
Is my report to his great worthiness.   63
ROSALINE
Another of these students at that time
Was there with him, if I have heard a truth.
Berowne they call him, but a merrier man,
Within the limit of becoming mirth,   67
I never spent an hour's talk withal.   68
His eye begets occasion for his wit,
For every object that the one doth catch   70
The other turns to a mirth-moving jest,
Which his fair tongue, conceit's expositor,   72
Delivers in such apt and gracious words,
That agèd ears play truant at his tales,   74
And younger hearings are quite ravishèd,

------

57 *Of . . . loved* loved for his virtue by all who love virtue   58 *Most . . . ill*
(Dumaine has the greatest ability to do harm but the least knowledge of evil)
59–60 *he . . . wit* he has the intelligence to compensate for a bad figure and a
physique to win favor even if he were stupid   62 *little* short   63 *to* compared with, in view of   67 *becoming* decorous   68 *withal* with   72 *conceit's
expositor* fancy's interpreter   74 *play truant* i.e., neglect serious matters

76   So sweet and voluble is his discourse.
PRINCESS
      God bless my ladies! Are they all in love,
      That every one her own hath garnishèd
      With such bedecking ornaments of praise?
LORD
80   Here comes Boyet.
            Enter Boyet.
PRINCESS   Now, what admittance, lord?
BOYET
      Navarre had notice of your fair approach;
82   And he and his competitors in oath
83   Were all addressed to meet you, gentle lady,
      Before I came. Marry, thus much I have learnt:
      He rather means to lodge you in the field,
      Like one that comes here to besiege his court,
      Than seek a dispensation for his oath
88   To let you enter his unpeopled house.
            Enter [the King of] Navarre, Longaville, Dumaine,
            and Berowne.
      Here comes Navarre.
90 KING   Fair princess, welcome to the court of Navarre.
PRINCESS   "Fair" I give you back again, and "welcome" I
92   have not yet. The roof of this court is too high to be
      yours, and welcome to the wide fields too base to be
      mine.
KING
      You shall be welcome, madam, to my court.
PRINCESS
      I will be welcome, then. Conduct me thither.
KING
      Hear me, dear lady – I have sworn an oath.
PRINCESS
      Our Lady help my lord! he'll be forsworn.

---

76 *voluble* fluent 80 *admittance* reception 82 *competitors* partners 83
addressed prepared 88 *unpeopled* without servants 92 *roof . . . court* i.e.,
the heavens

KING
>Not for the world, fair madam, by my will.   99
PRINCESS
>Why, will shall break it – will, and nothing else.   100
KING
>Your ladyship is ignorant what it is.
PRINCESS
>Were my lord so, his ignorance were wise,
>Where now his knowledge must prove ignorance.   103
>I hear your grace hath sworn out housekeeping: 104
>'Tis deadly sin to keep that oath, my lord,
>And sin to break it.
>But pardon me, I am too sudden-bold:
>To teach a teacher ill beseemeth me.
>Vouchsafe to read the purpose of my coming,
>And suddenly resolve me in my suit.   110
>   *[Gives a paper.]*
KING
>Madam, I will, if suddenly I may.
PRINCESS
>You will the sooner that I were away,   112
>For you'll prove perjured if you make me stay.
BEROWNE
>Did not I dance with you in Brabant once?
ROSALINE
>Did not I dance with you in Brabant once?
BEROWNE
>I know you did.
ROSALINE   How needless was it then
>To ask the question!
BEROWNE   You must not be so quick.
ROSALINE
>'Tis 'long of you that spur me with such questions.   118

---

99 *by my will* willingly   100 *will* desire   103 *Where* whereas   104 *sworn out housekeeping* sworn away hospitality   110 *suddenly resolve* quickly dispatch   112 *that . . . away* to procure my absence   118 *'long* because

BEROWNE
　　Your wit's too hot, it speeds too fast, 'twill tire.
ROSALINE
120　Not till it leave the rider in the mire.
BEROWNE
　　What time o' day?
ROSALINE
　　The hour that fools should ask.
BEROWNE
123　Now fair befall your mask!
ROSALINE
124　Fair fall the face it covers!
BEROWNE
　　And send you many lovers!
ROSALINE
　　Amen, so you be none.
BEROWNE
　　Nay, then will I be gone.
KING
128　Madam, your father here doth intimate
　　The payment of a hundred thousand crowns,
130　Being but the one half of an entire sum
131　Disbursèd by my father in his wars.
132　But say that he, or we (as neither have),
　　Received that sum, yet there remains unpaid
　　A hundred thousand more, in surety of the which,
　　One part of Aquitaine is bound to us,
136　Although not valued to the money's worth.
　　If then the king your father will restore
　　But that one half which is unsatisfied,
　　We will give up our right in Aquitaine,
140　And hold fair friendship with his majesty.
　　But that, it seems, he little purposeth,

---

123 *fair befall* good luck to　**124** *fall* befall　**128–29** *doth intimate / The payment* implies he has paid　**131** *his* (King of France's)　**132** *he* (Navarre's father)　**136** *valued* equal in value

For here he doth demand to have repaid   142
A hundred thousand crowns, and not demands,   143
On payment of a hundred thousand crowns,
To have his title live in Aquitaine,
Which we much rather had depart withal   146
And have the money by our father lent,
Than Aquitaine, so gelded as it is.   148
Dear princess, were not his requests so far
From reason's yielding, your fair self should make   *150*
A yielding 'gainst some reason in my breast,   151
And go well satisfied to France again.

PRINCESS
You do the king my father too much wrong,
And wrong the reputation of your name,
In so unseeming to confess receipt   155
Of that which hath so faithfully been paid.   156

KING
I do protest I never heard of it;
And if you prove it, I'll repay it back
Or yield up Aquitaine.   159

PRINCESS   We arrest your word.
Boyet, you can produce acquittances   *160*
For such a sum from special officers
Of Charles his father.

KING   Satisfy me so.

BOYET
So please your grace, the packet is not come
Where that and other specialties are bound.   164
Tomorrow you shall have a sight of them.

KING
It shall suffice me — at which interview

---

142 *demand to have repaid* claim to have already paid back   143 *and not de-*
mands i.e., instead of demanding   146 *depart* surrender   148 *gelded*
maimed, stripped   151 *A . . . reason* i.e., a fairly reasonable yielding (as
compared with the totally unreasonable one proposed by her father)   155
unseeming not seeming   156 *that* (the 200,000 crowns)   159 *arrest* seize as
hostage   164 *specialties* legal documents

167 All liberal reason I will yield unto.
Meantime, receive such welcome at my hand
As honor, without breach of honor, may
170 Make tender of to thy true worthiness.
You may not come, fair princess, within my gates,
But here without you shall be so received
173 As you shall deem yourself lodged in my heart,
Though so denied fair harbor in my house.
Your own good thoughts excuse me, and farewell.
Tomorrow shall we visit you again.

PRINCESS
177 Sweet health and fair desires consort your grace.

KING
Thy own wish wish I thee in every place.

Exit [with Longaville and Dumaine].

BEROWNE   Lady, I will commend you to mine own heart.
180 ROSALINE   Pray you, do my commendations; I would be
glad to see it.

BEROWNE   I would you heard it groan.
183 ROSALINE   Is the fool sick?

BEROWNE   Sick at the heart.

ROSALINE
185 Alack, let it blood.

BEROWNE
Would that do it good?

ROSALINE
My physic says "ay."

BEROWNE
Will you prick't with your eye?

ROSALINE
189 *Non point,* with my knife.

BEROWNE
190 Now, God save thy life.

---

167 *liberal* genteel   **170** *tender* offer   **173** *As* that   **177** *consort* dwell with
183 *fool* (a common term of affection or humorous abuse)   **185** *let it blood*
i.e., cure it by bleeding   **189** *Non point* (1) not at all, (2) it's blunt

ROSALINE
  And yours – from long living.
BEROWNE
  I cannot stay thanksgiving.   *Exit.*
    Enter Dumaine.
DUMAINE
  Sir, I pray you a word: what lady is that same?
BOYET
  The heir of Alençon, Katherine her name.
DUMAINE
  A gallant lady. Monsieur, fare you well.   *Exit.*
    [Enter Longaville.]
LONGAVILLE
  I beseech you a word: what is she in the white?
BOYET
  A woman sometimes, an you saw her in the light.   197
LONGAVILLE
  Perchance light in the light. I desire her name.   198
BOYET
  She hath but one for herself; to desire that were a shame.
LONGAVILLE
  Pray you, sir, whose daughter?   *200*
BOYET
  Her mother's, I have heard.
LONGAVILLE
  God's blessing on your beard!
BOYET
  Good sir, be not offended.
  She is an heir of Fauconbridge.
LONGAVILLE
  Nay, my choler is ended.
  She is a most sweet lady.
BOYET
  Not unlike, sir; that may be.   *Exit Longaville.*
    Enter Berowne.

---

197 *an* if **198** *light . . . light* i.e., wanton, if clearly seen

BEROWNE
   What's her name in the cap?
BOYET
   Rosaline, by good hap.
BEROWNE
210 Is she wedded or no?
BOYET
   To her will, sir, or so.
BEROWNE
   O, you are welcome, sir. Adieu.
BOYET
213 Farewell to me, sir, and welcome to you. *Exit Berowne.*
MARIA
   That last is Berowne, the merry madcap lord.
   Not a word with him but a jest.
BOYET   And every jest but a
      word.
PRINCESS
216 It was well done of you to take him at his word.
BOYET
   I was as willing to grapple, as he was to board.
KATHERINE
   Two hot sheeps, marry!
BOYET   And wherefore not ships?
   No sheep, sweet lamb, unless we feed on your lips.
KATHERINE
220 You sheep, and I pasture: shall that finish the jest?
BOYET
   So you grant pasture for me.
KATHERINE   Not so, gentle beast.
222 My lips are no common, though several they be.

---

213 *Farewell . . . you* i.e., I welcome your farewell 216 *take . . . word* i.e.,
contend with him at wordplay 220 *pasture* (a play on "pastor," meaning
shepherd) 222 *common* common grazing ground (i.e., available to any
man); *though* since; *several* two lips (with play on "several" as "more than
one," "parted," and in the legal sense of private lands as opposed to common
lands)

BOYET
  Belonging to whom?
KATHERINE   To my fortunes and me.
PRINCESS
  Good wits will be jangling; but, gentles, agree.
  This civil war of wits were much better used
  On Navarre and his bookmen, for here 'tis abused.   226
BOYET
  If my observation (which very seldom lies)
  By the heart's still rhetoric disclosèd with eyes   228
  Deceive me not now, Navarre is infected.
PRINCESS   With what?   *230*
BOYET
  With that which we lovers entitle affected.   231
PRINCESS   Your reason?
BOYET
  Why, all his behaviors did make their retire   233
  To the court of his eye, peeping thorough desire.   234
  His heart, like an agate, with your print impressed,   235
  Proud with his form, in his eye pride expressed.   236
  His tongue, all impatient to speak and not see,   237
  Did stumble with haste in his eyesight to be;   238
  All senses to that sense did make their repair,
  To feel only looking on fairest of fair.   240
  Methought all his senses were locked in his eye,
  As jewels in crystal for some prince to buy,
  Who, tend'ring their own worth from where they were   243
    glassed,
  Did point you to buy them, along as you passed.   244

---

226 *abused* misused 228 *still rhetoric* silent language 231 *affected* being moved by passion 233 *behaviors* attitudes 234 *thorough* through 235 *agate* (initials and designs were commonly engraved – *impressed* – on agates) 236 *with his* with its; *pride* i.e., the eye was proud of the privilege of holding your image 237 *all . . . see* i.e., impatient at being a speaking rather than a seeing organ 238 *in . . . be* i.e., to share the sight of the eyes 240 *To feel only* i.e., to concentrate on 243 *Who, tend'ring* which, offering; *glassed* encased in the crystal of his eyes 244 *point* indicate, invite

245   His face's own margin did quote such amazes,
        That all eyes saw his eyes enchanted with gazes.
247   I'll give you Aquitaine, and all that is his,
248   An you give him for my sake but one loving kiss.
PRINCESS
249   Come to our pavilion. Boyet is disposed.
BOYET
250   But to speak that in words which his eye hath disclosed.
        I only have made a mouth of his eye,
        By adding a tongue which I know will not lie.
MARIA
        Thou art an old lovemonger, and speakest skillfully.
KATHERINE
        He is Cupid's grandfather, and learns news of him.
ROSALINE
255   Then was Venus like her mother, for her father is but
            grim.
BOYET
        Do you hear, my mad wenches?
MARIA   No.
BOYET   What, then, do you
            see?
MARIA
        Ay, our way to be gone.
BOYET   You are too hard for me.
                                            Exeunt omnes.

                            *

---

245 *His . . . amazes* i.e., his amazed expression was a commentary on what
his eyes beheld (commentaries or glosses were often printed in the margin of
books)   247 *I'll give you* i.e., you can have   248 *An* if   249 *disposed* i.e., in
the mood (to be merry)   255 (Venus was Cupid's mother and looks nothing
like her "father," Boyet)

‰ **III.1** *Enter [Armado the] Braggart, and [Moth,] his Boy.*

ARMADO   Warble, child; make passionate my sense of   1
hearing.
MOTH   *[Sings.]* Concolinel.   3
ARMADO   Sweet air! Go, tenderness of years, take this
key, give enlargement to the swain, bring him festi-   5
nately hither. I must employ him in a letter to my love.
MOTH   Master, will you win your love with a French
brawl?   8
ARMADO   How meanest thou? Brawling in French?
MOTH   No, my complete master, but to jig off a tune at   10
the tongue's end, canary to it with your feet, humor it   11
with turning up your eyelids, sigh a note and sing a
note, sometime through the throat as if you swallowed
love with singing love, sometime through the nose as if
you snuffed up love by smelling love, with your hat
penthouse-like o'er the shop of your eyes, with your   16
arms crossed on your thin-belly doublet like a rabbit on   17
a spit, or your hands in your pocket like a man after the
old painting, and keep not too long in one tune, but a   19
snip and away. These are complements, these are hu-   20
mors, these betray nice wenches (that would be be-   21
trayed without these), and make them men of note –
do you note? – men that most are affected to these.   23
ARMADO   How hast thou purchased this experience?
MOTH   By my penny of observation.
ARMADO   But O – but O –   26

III.1   **1** *make passionate* render responsive   **3** *Concolinel* (unidentified; possibly the Irish song "Can cailin gheal," "Sing, maiden fair")   **5–6** *festinately*
quickly   **8** *brawl* a figure dance   **11** *canary* a lively Spanish dance   **16** *pent-
house* an overhang, such as often sheltered shops   **17** *on . . . doublet* i.e., on
the doublet covering your thin belly   **19** *old painting* (unidentified)   **20**
snip snippet, scrap; *complements* accomplishments   **20–21** *humors* manner-
isms   **21** *nice* coy   **23** *affected* drawn, given   **26–27** *But O . . . forgot* (re-
frain of a popular song; the hobbyhorse was a man dressed as a horse in rural
festive dances)

27 MOTH   The hobbyhorse is forgot.

ARMADO   Call'st thou my love "hobbyhorse"?

MOTH   No, master, the hobbyhorse is but a colt, and
30 your love perhaps a hackney. But have you forgot your
love?

ARMADO   Almost I had.

MOTH   Negligent student! learn her by heart.

ARMADO   By heart, and in heart, boy.

MOTH   And out of heart, master. All those three I will
prove.

ARMADO   What wilt thou prove?

MOTH   A man, if I live; and this, "by," "in," and "without," upon the instant. By heart you love her, because
40 your heart cannot come by her; in heart you love her,
because your heart is in love with her; and out of heart
you love her, being out of heart that you cannot enjoy
her.

ARMADO   I am all these three.

MOTH   *[Aside]* And three times as much more, and yet
nothing at all.

47 ARMADO   Fetch hither the swain. He must carry me a
letter.

49 MOTH   *[Aside]* A message well sympathized – a horse to
50 be ambassador for an ass.

ARMADO   Ha, ha? what sayest thou?

MOTH   Marry, sir, you must send the ass upon the horse,
for he is very slow-gaited. But I go.

ARMADO   The way is but short. Away!

MOTH   As swift as lead, sir.

ARMADO
The meaning, pretty ingenious?
Is not lead a metal heavy, dull, and slow?

MOTH
58 *Minime,* honest master, or rather, master, no.

27–30 *hobbyhorse, colt, hackney* (cant terms for prostitutes)   47 *me* for me
49 *sympathized* harmonized   58 *Minime* by no means (Latin)

ARMADO
  I say, lead is slow.
MOTH   You are too swift, sir, to say so.
  Is that lead slow which is fired from a gun?   60
ARMADO
  Sweet smoke of rhetoric!   61
  He reputes me a cannon, and the bullet, that's he.
  I shoot thee at the swain.   63
MOTH   Thump, then, and I flee.
                           [Exit.]

ARMADO
  A most acute juvenal; voluble and free of grace!   64
  By thy favor, sweet welkin, I must sigh in thy face.   65
  Most rude melancholy, valor gives thee place.   66
  My herald is returned.
    Enter [Moth the] Page, and [Costard the] Clown.
MOTH
  A wonder, master! Here's a costard broken in a shin.   68
ARMADO
  Some enigma, some riddle. Come, thy *l'envoi* – begin.   69
COSTARD   No egma, no riddle, no *l'envoi;* no salve in the   70
  mail, sir. O, sir, plantain, a plain plantain. No *l'envoi,*   71
  no *l'envoi,* no salve, sir, but a plantain.
ARMADO   By virtue, thou enforcest laughter; thy silly
  thought, my spleen; the heaving of my lungs provokes   74
  me to ridiculous smiling. O, pardon me, my stars!
  Doth the inconsiderate take salve for *l'envoi,* and the   76
  word *l'envoi* for a salve?

---

61 *smoke* product, essence   63 *Thump* (equivalent to "bang")   64 *juvenal*
youth   65 *By thy favor* with your permission; *welkin* sky   66 *gives thee place*
gives place to you – i.e., to melancholy   68 *costard* apple or head (and hence
having no shin)   69 *l'envoi* (usually a postscript to the reader at the end of a
literary work; here, an explanation)   70 *egma* (Costard's attempt at
"enigma"); *salve* (the play seems to be on "salve" – suggested by *l'envoi,* as
"farewell"; "salve," ointment, is a monosyllable; *salve,* the Latin word for
"greetings," is a disyllable)   71 *mail* pouch (such as might be carried by a
salve vendor or quacksalver); *plantain* a homely herbal remedy for broken
shins   74 *spleen* risibility (laughter supposedly originated in the spleen)   76
inconsiderate i.e., unthinking one

MOTH
   Do the wise think them other? Is not *l'envoi* a salve?
ARMADO
   No, page, it is an epilogue or discourse to make plain
80   Some obscure precedence that hath tofore been sain.
   I will example it:
82   The fox, the ape, and the humblebee
          Were still at odds, being but three.
   There's the moral. Now the *l'envoi*.
MOTH   I will add the *l'envoi*. Say the moral again.
ARMADO
        The fox, the ape, and the humblebee
          Were still at odds, being but three.
MOTH
        Until the goose came out of door,
89   And stayed the odds by adding four.
90   Now will I begin your moral, and do you follow with
   my *l'envoi*.
        The fox, the ape, and the humblebee
          Were still at odds, being but three.
ARMADO
94   Until the goose came out of door,
         Staying the odds by adding four.
96 MOTH   A good *l'envoi*, ending in the goose. Would you
   desire more?
COSTARD
98   The boy hath sold him a bargain, a goose – that's flat.
99   Sir, your pennyworth is good, an your goose be fat.
100 To sell a bargain well is as cunning as fast and loose.
   Let me see – a fat *l'envoi* – ay, that's a fat goose.

---

80 *precedence* preceding discourse; *sain* said **82** *humblebee* bumblebee **89** *stayed* wiped out; *four* a fourth **94** *goose* i.e., Armado (who has been tricked into the role) **96** *ending . . . goose* (because *envoi* ends with the sound "oie," "goose" in French) **98** *sold . . . bargain* i.e., outwitted him **99** *your . . . good* i.e., you got your money's worth; *an* if **100** *fast and loose* (cf. I.2.150)

ARMADO
    Come hither, come hither. How did this argument   102
    begin?
MOTH
    By saying that a costard was broken in a shin.
    Then called you for the *l'envoi.*
COSTARD
    True, and I for a plantain; thus came your argument in,
    Then the boy's fat *l'envoi,* the goose that you bought,
    And he ended the market.   107
ARMADO   But tell me, how was there a costard broken in
    a shin?
MOTH   I will tell you sensibly.   110
COSTARD   Thou hast no feeling of it, Moth. I will speak
    that *l'envoi:*
    I, Costard, running out, that was safely within,
    Fell over the threshold and broke my shin.
ARMADO   We will talk no more of this matter.
COSTARD   Till there be more matter in the shin.   116
ARMADO   Sirrah Costard, I will enfranchise thee.   117
COSTARD   O, marry me to one Frances! I smell some   118
    l'envoi, some goose, in this.
ARMADO   By my sweet soul, I mean setting thee at lib- *120*
    erty, enfreedoming thy person. Thou wert immured,   *121*
    restrained, captivated, bound.
COSTARD   True, true, and now you will be my purgation   123
    and let me loose.   124
ARMADO   I give thee thy liberty, set thee from durance,
    and in lieu thereof, impose on thee nothing but this.
    [Gives a letter.] Bear this significant to the country   127
    maid, Jaquenetta. *[Gives money.]* There is remunera-

---

102 *argument* topic, theme   **107** (alluding to the proverb "Three women
and a goose make a market")   **110** *sensibly* feelingly   **116** *matter* pus   **117**
enfranchise free   **118** *marry . . . Frances* (hearing Armado as having said "en-
Frances thee")   **121** *immured* imprisoned   **123** *purgation* enema (to free
him from constipation)   **124** *loose* shit   **127** *significant* communication

129   tion, for the best ward of mine honor is rewarding my
130   dependents. Moth, follow.   *[Exit.]*

MOTH
   Like the sequel, I. Señor Costard, adieu.   *Exit.*

COSTARD
132   My sweet ounce of man's flesh, my incony Jew!
   Now will I look to his remuneration. Remuneration?
   O, that's the Latin word for three farthings. Three far-
135   things – remuneration. "What's the price of this inkle?"
   "One penny," "No, I'll give you a remuneration." Why,
137   it carries it! Remuneration! Why, it is a fairer name
138   than French crown. I will never buy and sell out of this
   word.

     Enter Berowne.

140 BEROWNE   My good knave Costard, exceedingly well
   met.

142 COSTARD   Pray you, sir, how much carnation ribbon may
   a man buy for a remuneration?

BEROWNE   What is a remuneration?

COSTARD   Marry, sir, halfpenny farthing.

BEROWNE   Why then, three-farthing-worth of silk.

COSTARD   I thank your worship. God be wi' you.

BEROWNE   Stay, slave. I must employ thee.
   As thou wilt win my favor, good my knave,
150   Do one thing for me that I shall entreat.

COSTARD   When would you have it done, sir?

BEROWNE   This afternoon.

COSTARD   Well, I will do it, sir. Fare you well.

BEROWNE   Thou knowest not what it is.

COSTARD   I shall know, sir, when I have done it.

BEROWNE   Why, villain, thou must know first.

COSTARD   I will come to your worship tomorrow morn-
   ing.

---

129 *ward* defense   **132** *incony* darling; *Jew* (a term of playful abuse, perhaps
suggested by "*ju*venile")   **135** *inkle* tape   **137** *carries it* takes the prize   **138**
French crown (a coin, frequently associated with jests about venereal disease);
out of i.e., without using   **142** *carnation* flesh-colored

BEROWNE   It must be done this afternoon. Hark, slave, it
   is but this: *160*
   The princess comes to hunt here in the park,
   And in her train there is a gentle lady –
   When tongues speak sweetly, then they name her name,
   And Rosaline they call her. Ask for her,
   And to her white hand see thou do commend
   This sealed-up counsel. *[Gives letter and a shilling.]*   166
      There's thy guerdon: go.
COSTARD   Gardon, O sweet gardon! Better than remu-
   neration – elevenpence farthing better. Most sweet gar-
   don! I will do it, sir, in print. Gardon – remuneration.   169
                                                            Exit.

BEROWNE
   And I, forsooth, in love!   *170*
   I, that have been love's whip,
   A very beadle to a humorous sigh,   172
   A critic, nay, a night-watch constable,
   A domineering pedant o'er the boy,   174
   Than whom no mortal so magnificent.
   This wimpled, whining, purblind, wayward boy,   176
   This signor-junior, giant-dwarf, Dan Cupid,   177
   Regent of love rhymes, lord of folded arms,   178
   The anointed sovereign of sighs and groans,
   Liege of all loiterers and malcontents,   180
   Dread prince of plackets, king of codpieces,   181
   Sole imperator and great general   182
   Of trotting paritors – O my little heart!   183
   And I to be a corporal of his field,   184

---

166 *counsel* private message; *guerdon* reward   169 *in print* i.e., to the letter
172 *beadle . . . sigh* i.e., an officer of correction to moody symptoms of love
174 *pedant* schoolmaster   176 *wimpled* blindfolded; *purblind* wholly blind
177 *signor* (punning on "senior"); *Dan* don, sir (from "dominus")   178
folded arms (traditional posture of the melancholy lover)   180 *Liege* lord
181 *plackets* slits in petticoats (hence, female genitals); *codpieces* padded gus-
sets at the crotch of breeches (hence, penises)   182 *imperator* governor   183
paritors minor officers of ecclesiastical courts who profited by spying out sexual offenses   184 *corporal of his field* field officer

185 And wear his colors like a tumbler's hoop!
 What? I love, I sue, I seek a wife!
 A woman that is like a German clock,
188 Still a-repairing, ever out of frame,
 And never going aright, being a watch,
190 But being watched that it may still go right!
 Nay, to be perjured, which is worst of all,
 And, among three, to love the worst of all,
193 A whitely wanton with a velvet brow,
194 With two pitch balls stuck in her face for eyes.
195 Ay, and, by heaven, one that will do the deed,
196 Though Argus were her eunuch and her guard.
197 And I to sigh for her, to watch for her,
 To pray for her! Go to, it is a plague
 That Cupid will impose for my neglect
200 Of his almighty dreadful little might.
 Well, I will love, write, sigh, pray, sue, groan:
202 Some men must love my lady, and some Joan. *[Exit.]*

*

∾ **IV.1** *Enter the Princess, a Forester, her Ladies [Maria,*
  Katherine, Rosaline], and her Lords [Boyet and others].

PRINCESS
 Was that the king that spurred his horse so hard
 Against the steep uprising of the hill?
BOYET
 I know not, but I think it was not he.
PRINCESS
4 Whoe'er a was, a showed a mounting mind.

---

185 *tumbler's hoop* (an object conspicuously beribboned) **188** *frame* order
193 *whitely* pale-skinned; *velvet* smooth **194** *pitch* tar-black **195** *do the
deed* have sex **196** *Argus* in mythology a monster with a hundred eyes; *eunuch* guard in a seraglio **197** *watch* stay awake **202** *Joan* (proverbial name
for a lower-class woman)
 IV.1 **4** *a* he; *mounting* aspiring

Well, lords, today we shall have our dispatch.
On Saturday we will return to France.
Then, forester, my friend, where is the bush
That we must stand and play the murderer in?
FORESTER
Hereby, upon the edge of yonder coppice,
A stand where you may make the fairest shoot.   10
PRINCESS
I thank my beauty, I am fair that shoot,
And thereupon thou speak'st the fairest shoot.
FORESTER
Pardon me, madam, for I meant not so.
PRINCESS
What, what? First praise me, and again say no?
O short-lived pride! Not fair? Alack for woe!
FORESTER
Yes, madam, fair.   16
PRINCESS   Nay, never paint me now:
Where fair is not, praise cannot mend the brow.   17
Here, good my glass, take this for telling true –   18
    [Gives money.]
Fair payment for foul words is more than due.
FORESTER
Nothing but fair is that which you inherit.   20
PRINCESS
See, see – my beauty will be saved by merit.   21
O heresy in fair, fit for these days,   22
A giving hand, though foul, shall have fair praise.
But come, the bow. Now mercy goes to kill,   24
And shooting well is then accounted ill.
Thus will I save my credit in the shoot:
Not wounding, pity would not let me do't;

---

10 *stand* concealed position toward which the game was driven; *fairest* best
16 *paint* flatter   17 *brow* i.e., face   18 *good my glass* my good mirror   20
inherit possess   21 *merit* i.e., good works, the "alms" she has given the
forester   22 *heresy* (in orthodox Anglican doctrine salvation came by faith
rather than by good works)   24 *mercy* i.e., the merciful princess

If wounding, then it was to show my skill,
29 That more for praise than purpose meant to kill.
30 And out of question so it is sometimes,
31 Glory grows guilty of detested crimes,
32 When, for fame's sake, for praise, an outward part,
33 We bend to that the working of the heart,
As I for praise alone now seek to spill
The poor deer's blood, that my heart means no ill.

BOYET
36 Do not curst wives hold that self-sovereignty
Only for praise' sake, when they strive to be
Lords o'er their lords?

PRINCESS
Only for praise, and praise we may afford
40 To any lady that subdues a lord.
   Enter [Costard the] Clown.

BOYET
41 Here comes a member of the commonwealth.

42 COSTARD God dig-you-den all. Pray you, which is the
head lady?

PRINCESS Thou shalt know her, fellow, by the rest that
have no heads.

COSTARD Which is the greatest lady, the highest?

PRINCESS The thickest and the tallest.

COSTARD The thickest and the tallest – it is so. Truth is
truth.

50 An your waist, mistress, were as slender as my wit,
One o' these maids' girdles for your waist should be fit.
Are not you the chief woman? You are the thickest here.

PRINCESS What's your will, sir? What's your will?

COSTARD I have a letter from Monsieur Berowne to one
Lady Rosaline.

---

29 *That . . . kill* i.e., who shot well to win praise rather than from any desire
to strike the deer 31 *Glory . . . of* i.e., desire for glory is responsible for 32
an outward part a superficial thing 33 *bend* adapt 36 *curst* shrewish; *self-
sovereignty* self-rule (instead of rule by their husbands) 41 *commonwealth*
common people 42 *dig-you-den* give you good evening

PRINCESS
  O thy letter, thy letter! He's a good friend of mine.
  Stand aside, good bearer. Boyet, you can carve.   57
  Break up this capon.   58
BOYET   I am bound to serve.
  This letter is mistook; it importeth none here.   59
  It is writ to Jaquenetta.   60
PRINCESS   We will read it, I swear.
  Break the neck of the wax, and every one give ear.   61
BOYET   *Reads.* "By heaven, that thou art fair is most in-
  fallible, true that thou art beauteous, truth itself that
  thou art lovely. More fairer than fair, beautiful than
  beauteous, truer than truth itself, have commiseration
  on thy heroical vassal. The magnanimous and most
  illustrate King Cophetua set eye upon the pernicious   67
  and indubitate beggar Zenelophon, and he it was that   68
  might rightly say *veni, vidi, vici;* which to annothanize   69
  in the vulgar (O base and obscure vulgar!) videlicet, he   70
  came, see, and overcame. He came, one; see, two; over-   71
  came, three. Who came? The king. Why did he come?
  To see. Why did he see? To overcome. To whom came
  he? To the beggar. What saw he? The beggar. Who
  overcame he? The beggar. The conclusion is victory.
  On whose side? The king's. The captive is enriched. On
  whose side? The beggar's. The catastrophe is a nuptial.   77
  On whose side? The king's? No – on both in one, or
  one in both. I am the king (for so stands the comparison), thou the beggar (for so witnesseth thy lowliness).   80
  Shall I command thy love? I may. Shall I enforce thy
  love? I could. Shall I entreat thy love? I will. What shalt
  thou exchange for rags? Robes. For tittles? Titles. For   83

---

57 *carve* (1) cut meat, (2) make courtly gestures   58 *capon* love letter (from
French slang – *poulet*)   59 *importeth* concerns   61 *wax* seal   67 *illustrate* illustrious;   *pernicious*   (for   "penurious")   68   *indubitate*   indubitable;
Zenelophon (Penelophon, in the old ballad "King Cophetua and the Beggar-
maid")   69 *annothanize* anatomize, parse   70 *vulgar* vernacular; *videlicet*
that is to say   71 *see* saw   77 *catastrophe* denouement   83 *tittles* jots, parti-
cles

thyself? Me. Thus, expecting thy reply, I profane my
lips on thy foot, my eyes on thy picture, and my heart
on thy every part.

87   Thine in the dearest design of industry,
                              Don Adriano de Armado.
89   Thus dost thou hear the Nemean lion roar
90   'Gainst thee, thou lamb, that standest as his prey.
       Submissive fall his princely feet before,
92   And he from forage will incline to play.
       But if thou strive, poor soul, what art thou then?
94   Food for his rage, repasture for his den."

PRINCESS
95   What plume of feathers is he that indited this letter?
96   What vane? What weathercock? Did you ever hear better?

BOYET
       I am much deceived but I remember the style.

PRINCESS
98   Else your memory is bad, going o'er it erewhile.

BOYET
99   This Armado is a Spaniard that keeps here in court,
100   A phantasim, a Monarcho, and one that makes sport
       To the prince and his bookmates.

PRINCESS   Thou fellow, a word.
       Who gave thee this letter?

COSTARD   I told you – my lord.

PRINCESS
       To whom shouldst thou give it?

COSTARD   From my lord to my
       lady.

PRINCESS
       From which lord, to which lady?

---

87 *dearest . . . industry* i.e., best pattern of assiduous courtship   89 *Nemean lion* (slain by Hercules as the first of his labors)   92 *forage* foraging, ravaging   94 *repasture* repast   95 *plume of feathers* i.e., dandy, coxcomb   96 *vane* weather vane (with play on "vain")   98 *erewhile* just now   99 *keeps* dwells   100 *phantasim* one who indulges in fantasies; *Monarcho* (the nickname of an Italian eccentric whose delusions of grandeur entertained the English court for some years prior to 1580)

COSTARD
　From my lord Berowne, a good master of mine,
　To a lady of France, that he called Rosaline.

PRINCESS
　Thou hast mistaken his letter. Come, lords, away.　107
　　[To Rosaline]
　Here, sweet, put up this; 'twill be thine another day.　108
　　　　　　　Exeunt [Princess, Forester, and Attendants].

BOYET
　Who is the suitor? Who is the suitor?　109

ROSALINE　　　　　　　　　　　　Shall I teach you
　to know?

BOYET
　Ay, my continent of beauty.　110

ROSALINE　　　　　　　　　　Why, she that bears the
　bow.
　Finely put off!　111

BOYET
　My lady goes to kill horns, but, if thou marry,　112
　Hang me by the neck if horns that year miscarry.
　Finely put on!

ROSALINE
　Well then, I am the shooter.　115

BOYET　　　　　　　　　　And who is your deer?

ROSALINE
　If we choose by the horns, yourself. Come not near.
　Finely put on, indeed!

MARIA
　You still wrangle with her, Boyet, and she strikes at the　118
　brow.

BOYET
　But she herself is hit lower. Have I hit her now?　119

---

107 *mistaken* wrongly delivered　108 *'twill be thine* i.e., it will be your turn
109 *suitor* (pronounced "shooter")　110 *continent of* container of　111 *put
off* turned aside　112 *horns* i.e., a deer (followed by an allusion to the horns
of cuckoldry)　115 *deer* (punning on "dear")　118 *brow* (where he would
wear horns)　119 *lower* (heart or genitals); *hit her* scored a point with her

120 ROSALINE Shall I come upon thee with an old saying
121   that was a man when King Pepin of France was a little
    boy, as touching the "hit it"?
  BOYET So I may answer thee with one as old – that was
    a woman when Queen Guinever of Britain was a little
    wench, as touching the "hit it."
  ROSALINE
126   "Thou canst not hit it, hit it, hit it,
        Thou canst not hit it, my good man."
  BOYET
        "An I cannot, cannot, cannot,
        An I cannot, another can." *Exit [Rosaline].*
  COSTARD
130   By my troth, most pleasant, how both did fit it!
  MARIA
131   A mark marvelous well shot, for they both did hit it.
  BOYET
    A mark! (O mark but that mark!) A mark, says my lady!
133   Let the mark have a prick in't to mete at if it may be.
  MARIA
134   Wide o' the bow hand! I' faith your hand is out.
  COSTARD
135   Indeed a must shoot nearer, or he'll ne'er hit the clout.
  BOYET
136   An if my hand be out, then belike your hand is in.
  COSTARD
137   Then will she get the upshoot by cleaving the pin.

---

120 *come upon thee* confront you   121 *was a man* i.e., was old; *King Pepin* (Carlovingian king, Pépin III, who died in 768)   126–29 *Thou . . . can* (adapted from a bawdy song and dance of the period)   131 *mark* target   133 *mark have a prick in't* (1) target have a bull's-eye in it, (2) vagina have a penis in it; *mete at* measure by   134 *Wide . . . hand* too far left; *out* out of practice   135 *a* he; *shoot* ejaculate; *clout* (1) white-headed pin in the center of the target, (2) vagina   136 (1) if I'm out of practice at sex and archery, then probably you're an expert, (2) if I can't touch your vagina, then that's probably because you are masturbating   137 (1) she will get the leading shot in the archery (and wit) contest by splitting the bull's-eye, (2) she will make her lover ejaculate by squeezing his penis hard

MARIA

Come, come, you talk greasily; your lips grow foul.   138

COSTARD

She's too hard for you at pricks. Sir, challenge her to   139
bowl.

BOYET

I fear too much rubbing. Good night, my good owl.   140

[Exeunt Boyet and Maria.]

COSTARD

By my soul, a swain, a most simple clown!

Lord, lord, how the ladies and I have put him down!

O' my troth, most sweet jests, most incony vulgar wit!   143

When it comes so smoothly off, so obscenely as it were,   144
so fit.

Armado o' th' t' other side – O, a most dainty man!   145

To see him walk before a lady, and to bear her fan,

To see him kiss his hand, and how most sweetly a will
swear,

And his page o' t' other side, that handful of wit,

Ah, heavens, it is a most pathetical nit!   149

Shout within.

Sola, sola!   *[Exit.]*   150

*

---

138 *greasily* smuttily   **139** (1) She's too good for you at archery. Sir, challenge her to a game of bowls instead, (2) She's too difficult to penetrate with
a penis. Sir, ask her to masturbate you instead; *pricks* (1) informal or illegal
archery, (2) penises   **140** *rubbing* (a "rub" was an obstacle between bowler
and jack in bowls; also "masturbating"); *owl* (a night bird; a pun on "ole" [=
"hole," vagina])   **143** *incony* darling; *vulgar* obscene   **144** *obscenely* (uncon-
sciously apt malapropism – for "seemly"?)   **145–49** *Armado . . . nit* (editors
often assume these lines are misplaced, but Costard is contrasting the dirty
jokes with Armado; *o' th' t' other side* on the other hand)   **149** *pathetical nit*
pleasing mite   **150** *Sola, sola* (a hunting cry)

ᴥ **IV.2** *Enter Dull, Holofernes the Pedant, and
Nathaniel.*

1 NATHANIEL Very reverend sport, truly, and done in the
testimony of a good conscience.

3 HOLOFERNES The deer was, as you know, *sanguis,* in
4 blood, ripe as the pomewater, who now hangeth like a
jewel in the ear of *caelo,* the sky, the welkin, the heaven;
6 and anon falleth like a crab on the face of *terra,* the soil,
the land, the earth.

    NATHANIEL Truly, Master Holofernes, the epithets are
9 sweetly varied, like a scholar at the least; but sir, I assure
10 ye it was a buck of the first head.

11 HOLOFERNES Sir Nathaniel, *haud credo.*

12 DULL 'Twas not a old gray doe; 'twas a pricket.

13 HOLOFERNES Most barbarous intimation! Yet a kind of
14 insinuation, as it were, *in via,* in way, of explication;
15 *facere,* as it were, replication, or rather, *ostentare,* to
show, as it were, his inclination – after his undressed,
unpolished, uneducated, unpruned, untrained, or,
rather, unlettered, or, ratherest, unconfirmed fashion –
19 to insert again my *haud credo* for a deer.

20 DULL I said the deer was not a old gray doe – 'twas a
pricket.

IV.2 s.d. *Holofernes* (Gargantua's tutor in Rabelais's *Gargantua and Panta-
gruel* but also, in the Book of Judith in the Bible, Nebuchadnezzar's general,
decapitated by Judith) **1** *reverend* worthy of respect **1–2** *in the testimony*
with the warrant **3–4** *in blood* in prime condition **4** *pomewater* (a variety
of apple) **6** *crab* crab apple **9** *at the least* to say the least **10** *of . . . head* of
the fifth year (and therefore a *buck;* Holofernes has called it a *deer*) **11** *Sir*
dominus (term of address for a clergyman in minor orders); *haud credo* I do
not think so **12** *old gray doe* (Dull's mishearing of *haud credo*); *pricket* male
deer of the second year **13** *intimation* intrusion **14** *insinuation* interpreta-
tion **15** *facere . . . replication* to give another explanation **19** *insert* put in,
interpret

HOLOFERNES   Twice-sod simplicity, *bis coctus!*   22
O thou monster Ignorance, how deformèd dost thou
look!

NATHANIEL
Sir, he hath never fed of the dainties that are bred in a
book.
He hath not eat paper, as it were, he hath not drunk
ink, his intellect is not replenished, he is only an ani-
mal, only sensible in the duller parts.
And such barren plants are set before us that we thank-
ful should be,
Which we of taste and feeling are, for those parts that   29
do fructify in us more than he;
For as it would ill become me to be vain, indiscreet, or   30
a fool:
So were there a patch set on learning, to see him in a   31
school.
But, *omne bene,* say I, being of an old father's mind,   32
Many can brook the weather that love not the wind.   33

DULL
You two are bookmen. Can you tell me by your wit,
What was a month old at Cain's birth that's not five
weeks old as yet?

HOLOFERNES
Dictynna, goodman Dull. Dictynna, goodman Dull.   36
DULL   What is Dictynna?
NATHANIEL   A title to Phoebe, to Luna, to the moon.
HOLOFERNES
The moon was a month old when Adam was no more,
And raught not to five weeks when he came to fivescore.   40
Th' allusion holds in the exchange.   41

---

22 *sod* soaked; *bis coctus* twice-cooked   **29** *Which we* we who; *fructify* grow
fruitful; *he* in him   **31** *patch . . . learning* (1) disfigurement of education, (2)
clown put to school   **32** *omne bene* all's well; *father's* sage's   **33** *brook* put up
with – i.e., what can't be cured must be endured   **36** *Dictynna* Diana, the
moon   **40** *raught* reached   **41** *allusion* riddle; *exchange* substitution (of
Adam's name for Cain's)

42 DULL   'Tis true indeed; the collusion holds in the exchange.

HOLOFERNES   God comfort thy capacity! I say th' allusion holds in the exchange.

46 DULL   And I say the pollution holds in the exchange, for
the moon is never but a month old, and I say beside
that 'twas a pricket that the princess killed.

HOLOFERNES   Sir Nathaniel, will you hear an extemporal
50 epitaph on the death of the deer? And, to humor the ignorant, call I the deer the princess killed, a pricket.

52 NATHANIEL   *Perge,* good Master Holofernes, *perge,* so it
shall please you to abrogate scurrility.

54 HOLOFERNES   I will something affect the letter, for it ar-
gues facility.

The preyful princess pierced and pricked a pretty pleasing pricket;

57   Some say a sore, but not a sore till now made sore
with shooting.

58 The dogs did yell. Put "l" to "sore," then sorel jumps
from thicket –

59   Or pricket, sore, or else sorel. The people fall a-
hooting.

60 If sore be sore, then "l" to "sore" makes fifty sores – O
sore "l"!

61 Of one sore I an hundred make by adding but one
more "l."

NATHANIEL   A rare talent!

63 DULL   If a talent be a claw, look how he claws him with a
talent.

HOLOFERNES   This is a gift that I have, simple, simple, a
66 foolish extravagant spirit, full of forms, figures, shapes,

---

42, 46 *collusion, pollution* (Dull's errors for "allusion" hint at the verbal trick
in which Nathaniel and Holofernes collude and the "pollution" of English by
Latin)   52 *Perge* proceed   54 *affect the letter* i.e., lean to the use of alliteration
57 *sore* buck of the fourth year   58 *sorel* buck of the third year   59 *Or*
either   60 *l* Roman numeral fifty   61 (by spelling it "sorell")   63 *talent* i.e.,
talon; *claws* scratches, flatters   66 *extravagant* wandering

objects, ideas, apprehensions, motions, revolutions. 67
These are begot in the ventricle of memory, nourished 68
in the womb of pia mater, and delivered upon the mel- 69
lowing of occasion. But the gift is good in those in 70
whom it is acute, and I am thankful for it.

NATHANIEL Sir, I praise the Lord for you, and so may
my parishioners, for their sons are well tutored by you,
and their daughters profit very greatly under you. You 74
are a good member of the commonwealth.

HOLOFERNES *Mehercle,* if their sons be ingenious, they 76
shall want no instruction; if their daughters be capable, 77
I will put it to them. But, *vir sapit qui pauca loquitur.* A 78
soul feminine saluteth us.

Enter Jaquenetta and [Costard] the Clown.

JAQUENETTA God give you good morrow, Master Per- 80
son.

HOLOFERNES Master Person, *quasi* pierce one? And if 82
one should be pierced, which is the one? 83

COSTARD Marry, Master Schoolmaster, he that is likest
to a hogshead.

HOLOFERNES Of piercing a hogshead! A good luster of 86
conceit in a turf of earth, fire enough for a flint, pearl
enough for a swine – 'tis pretty, it is well.

JAQUENETTA Good Master Person, be so good as read
me this letter. It was given me by Costard, and sent me 90
from Don Armado. I beseech you read it.

---

67 *motions* impulses 67 *revolutions* reflections 68 *ventricle* (of the three
sections or "ventricles" of the brain, one was believed to contain the memory) 69 *womb of pia mater* center of the enclosing membrane or purse 74
under (the start of a series of sexual double meanings, continued with "member," "capable," "put it to them") 76 *Mehercle* by Hercules 77 *capable* (1)
able, (2) sexually mature (operating with other double entendres of the passage) 78 *vir . . . loquitur* the man is wise who speaks little 80–81 *Person*
(pronunciation of "parson") 82 *quasi* that is 83 *pierced* (pronounced
"persed") 86 *Of . . . hogshead* i.e., getting drunk 86–87 *luster of conceit*
gleam of fancy

92 HOLOFERNES *Facile precor gelida quando pecas omnia sub*
    umbra ruminat, and so forth. Ah, good old Mantuan. I
    may speak of thee as the traveler doth of Venice:
95   *Venezia, Venezia,*
            Que non te vide, que non te perrechia.
    Old Mantuan, old Mantuan! Who understandeth thee
98 not, loves thee not. Ut, re, sol, la, mi, fa. Under pardon,
    sir, what are the contents? or, rather, as Horace says in
100 his – What my soul! Verses?

NATHANIEL   Ay, sir, and very learned.

102 HOLOFERNES   Let me hear a staff, a stanze, a verse. *Lege,*
    domine.

NATHANIEL   *[Reads.]*
104   "If love make me forsworn, how shall I swear to love?
            Ah, never faith could hold if not to beauty vowed!
        Though to myself forsworn, to thee I'll faithful prove;
107   Those thoughts to me were oaks, to thee like osiers
                bowed.
108   Study his bias leaves and makes his book thine eyes,
            Where all those pleasures live that art would compre-
                hend.
110   If knowledge be the mark, to know thee shall suffice:
            Well learnèd is that tongue that well can thee com-
                mend,
        All ignorant that soul that sees thee without wonder;
113   Which is to me some praise, that I thy parts admire.

92–93 *Facile . . . ruminat* ("Easily, I pray, since you are getting everything
wrong under the cool shade, it ruminates," a misquotation of the opening of
the first eclogue of Mantuan [Italian poet, 1448–1516] – a common school
tag: *"Fauste, precor gelida quando pecus omne sub umbra ruminat,"* "Faustus, I
beg, while all the cattle ruminate beneath the cool shade." The errors,
though funny, may be the printer's or Holofernes' or Shakespeare's.) **95–96**
Venezia . . . perrechia (rugged form of an Italian proverb appearing in Florio's
First Fruits, 1578: "Venice, Venice, who loves you not sees you not") **98** *Ut*
(since replaced by "do"; Holofernes is incorrectly singing the scale) **102–3**
Lege, domine read, master **104–17** (a sonnet) **107** *thoughts . . . were* reso-
lutions that seemed to me **108** *his bias leaves* i.e., abandons its previous in-
clinations **113** *praise* credit, honor

Thy eye Jove's lightning bears, thy voice his dreadful
   thunder,
   Which, not to anger bent, is music and sweet fire.
Celestial as thou art, O pardon love this wrong,
That sings heaven's praise with such an earthly tongue!"
HOLOFERNES   You find not the apostrophus, and so miss   118
   the accent. Let me supervise the canzonet. Here are   119
   only numbers ratified; but, for the elegancy, facility,   120
   and golden cadence of poesy, *caret.* Ovidius Naso was   121
   the man; and why indeed "Naso" but for smelling out
   the odoriferous flowers of fancy, the jerks of invention?   123
   Imitari is nothing. So doth the hound his master, the   124
   ape his keeper, the tired horse his rider. But, *domicella* –   125
   virgin – was this directed to you?
JAQUENETTA   Ay, sir.   127
HOLOFERNES   I will overglance the superscript. "To the   128
   snow-white hand of the most beauteous Lady Ros-
   aline." I will look again on the intellect of the letter, for   130
   the nomination of the party writing to the person written unto. "Your ladyship's, in all desired employment,
   Berowne." Sir Nathaniel, this Berowne is one of the
   votaries with the king, and here he hath framed a letter
   to a sequent of the stranger queen's, which accidentally,   135
   or by the way of progression, hath miscarried. Trip and   136
   go, my sweet, deliver this paper into the royal hand of

118 *find* regard; *apostrophus* apostrophe (disregarding contractions indicated
by apostrophes can spoil the meter; but perhaps Holofernes is using learned
terms at random)   119 *supervise* look over; *canzonet* ditty   120 *numbers ratified* i.e., mechanical versification   121 *caret* it is lacking; *Naso* (from *nasus,*
nose)   123 *jerks of invention* strokes of wit   124 *Imitari* to imitate   125
tired spiritless (Holofernes seems to be linking imitativeness and docility)
127 (Q continues "from one mounsieur *Berowne,* one of the strange
Queenes Lordes," but Jaquenetta has said, ll. 90–91, it is from Don Armado;
Berowne is not one of the princess's lords, and Jaquenetta could not know
Berowne wrote the letter – the error is probably Shakespeare's)   128 *superscript* address   130 *intellect* purport   135 *sequent* follower; *queen's*
(Holofernes – or Shakespeare – gets the princess's title wrong)   136 *by* . . .
progression i.e., en route

138   the king; it may concern much. Stay not thy compli-
        ment; I forgive thy duty. Adieu.

140 JAQUENETTA   Good Costard, go with me. Sir, God save
        your life.

     COSTARD   Have with thee, my girl.

                             Exit [with Jaquenetta].

     NATHANIEL   Sir, you have done this in the fear of God
        very religiously; and, as a certain father saith –

145 HOLOFERNES   Sir, tell not me of the father; I do fear col-
        orable colors. But to return to the verses – did they
        please you, Sir Nathaniel?

148 NATHANIEL   Marvelous well for the pen.

     HOLOFERNES   I do dine today at the father's of a certain
150   pupil of mine, where, if before repast it shall please you
        to gratify the table with a grace, I will, on my privilege
        I have with the parents of the foresaid child or pupil,
153   undertake your *ben venuto,* where I will prove those
        verses to be very unlearned, neither savoring of poetry,
        wit, nor invention. I beseech your society.

     NATHANIEL   And thank you too, for society (saith the
157   text) is the happiness of life.

158 HOLOFERNES   And, certes, the text most infallibly con-
        cludes it. *[To Dull]* Sir, I do invite you too; you shall
160   not say me nay. *Pauca verba.* Away! The gentles are at
        their game, and we will to our recreation.   *Exeunt.*

                     *

∾ **IV.3**   *Enter Berowne with a paper in his hand, alone.*

     BEROWNE   The king he is hunting the deer; I am cours-
2   ing myself. They have pitched a toil; I am toiling in a
3   pitch – pitch that defiles. Defile – a foul word! Well, set

---

138–39 *Stay . . . compliment* i.e., do not stand on ceremony   145–46 *col-
orable colors* plausible pretexts   148 *pen* style (as contrasted with content)
153 *ben venuto* welcome   157 *text* (unidentified)   158 *certes* certainly (two
syllables)   160 *Pauca verba* few words
     IV.3   2 *pitched a toil* set a snare   3 *pitch* (Rosaline's eyes)   3–4 *set . . .
sorrow* (cf. I.1.298–99)

thee down, sorrow, for so they say the fool said, and so
say I, and I the fool. Well proved, wit! By the Lord, this
love is as mad as Ajax: it kills sheep; it kills me – I a 6
sheep. Well proved again o' my side! I will not love; if I
do, hang me. I' faith, I will not. O but her eye! By this
light, but for her eye, I would not love her – yes, for her
two eyes. Well, I do nothing in the world but lie, and 10
lie in my throat. By heaven, I do love, and it hath
taught me to rhyme, and to be melancholy; and here is
part of my rhyme, and here my melancholy. Well, she
hath one o' my sonnets already. The clown bore it, the
fool sent it, and the lady hath it – sweet clown, sweeter
fool, sweetest lady! By the world, I would not care a pin
if the other three were in. Here comes one with a paper: 17
God give him grace to groan! 18

    He stands aside.
    The King ent'reth [with a paper].

KING Ay me!
BEROWNE *[Aside]* Shot, by heaven! Proceed, sweet 20
  Cupid; thou hast thumped him with thy bird-bolt 21
  under the left pap. In faith, secrets! 22
KING *[Reads.]*
  "So sweet a kiss the golden sun gives not
    To those fresh morning drops upon the rose,
  As thy eyebeams when their fresh rays have smote
    The night of dew that on my cheeks down flows.
  Nor shines the silver moon one half so bright
    Through the transparent bosom of the deep
  As doth thy face, through tears of mine, give light.
    Thou shin'st in every tear that I do weep. 30
  No drop but as a coach doth carry thee;
    So ridest thou triumphing in my woe.
  Do but behold the tears that swell in me,

---

6 *Ajax* legendary Greek warrior who ran mad and mistook sheep for an army
after he failed to be awarded the armor of Achilles 17 *in* involved 18 s.d.
aside (by l. 75 he is on a higher level, "in the sky" – possibly in the gallery
over the stage) 20 *Proceed* i.e., rise in status 21 *bird-bolt* blunt arrow 22
left pap left breast (heart)

And they thy glory through my grief will show.
But do not love thyself – then thou will keep
36   My tears for glasses and still make me weep.
O queen of queens, how far dost thou excel
No thought can think, nor tongue of mortal tell!"
How shall she know my griefs? I'll drop the paper.
40   Sweet leaves, shade folly. Who is he comes here?
     Enter Longaville [with a paper]. The King steps aside.
What, Longaville? and reading? Listen, ear.
BEROWNE   *[Aside]*
42   Now, in thy likeness, one more fool appear!
LONGAVILLE
Ay me, I am forsworn.
BEROWNE   *[Aside]*
44   Why, he comes in like a perjure, wearing papers.
KING   *[Aside]*
In love, I hope – sweet fellowship in shame!
BEROWNE   *[Aside]*
One drunkard loves another of the name.
LONGAVILLE
Am I the first that have been perjured so?
BEROWNE   *[Aside]*
I could put thee in comfort – not by two that I know.
49   Thou mak'st the triumviry, the cornercap of society,
50   The shape of love's Tyburn, that hangs up simplicity.
LONGAVILLE
51   I fear these stubborn lines lack power to move.
O sweet Maria, empress of my love!
These numbers will I tear, and write in prose.

---

36 *glasses* mirrors   **40** *shade* conceal (the king is supposedly hiding behind a bush, probably represented by a stage pillar)   **42** *in thy likeness* looking like you   **44** *perjure* perjurer; *wearing papers* i.e., exposed in the stocks and wearing the papers involved in his offense   **49** *triumviry* triumvirate   **49–50** *cornercap . . . Tyburn* (an allusion to the three-cornered cap worn by Roman Catholic priests, such as Dr. Story, who was hanged at Tyburn in 1571 on gallows shaped as a triangle, and thereafter called "Dr. Story's cap")   **50** *simplicity* folly   **51** *stubborn* i.e., composed with difficulty

BEROWNE   *[Aside]*
  O, rhymes are guards on wanton Cupid's hose;   54
  Disfigure not his slop.   55
LONGAVILLE   This same shall go.
    He reads the sonnet.
  "Did not the heavenly rhetoric of thine eye,
    'Gainst whom the world cannot hold argument,
  Persuade my heart to this false perjury?
    Vows for thee broke deserve not punishment.
  A woman I forswore, but I will prove,   60
    Thou being a goddess, I forswore not thee.
  My vow was earthly, thou a heavenly love;
    Thy grace, being gained, cures all disgrace in me.   63
  Vows are but breath, and breath a vapor is:
    Then thou, fair sun, which on my earth dost shine,
  Exhal'st this vapor vow; in thee it is.   66
    If broken then, it is no fault of mine;
  If by me broke, what fool is not so wise
  To lose an oath to win a paradise?"
BEROWNE   *[Aside]*
  This is the liver vein, which makes flesh a deity,   70
  A green goose a goddess. Pure, pure idolatry.   71
  God amend us, God amend! We are much out o' th' way.   72
    Enter Dumaine [with a paper].
LONGAVILLE
  By whom shall I send this? – Company? Stay.
    [Steps aside.]
BEROWNE   *[Aside]*
  All hid, all hid – an old infant play.   74
  Like a demigod here sit I in the sky,
  And wretched fools' secrets heedfully o'ereye.
  More sacks to the mill – O heavens, I have my wish!   77

---

54 *guards* trimmings   55 *slop* breeches   63 *grace* favor   66 *Exhal'st* draws
up, absorbs   70 *liver vein* i.e., sentiment of the liver (organ of passion)   71
green goose i.e., gosling, young girl   72 *much . . . way* badly astray   74 *in-fant play* child's game   77 *More . . . mill* i.e., more work, more grain to be
ground

78   Dumaine transformed – four woodcocks in a dish!

DUMAINE
    O most divine Kate!

BEROWNE   *[Aside]*

80   O most profane coxcomb!

DUMAINE
    By heaven, the wonder in a mortal eye!

BEROWNE   *[Aside]*

82   By earth, she is not, corporal; there you lie.

DUMAINE

83   Her amber hairs for foul have amber quoted.

BEROWNE   *[Aside]*

84   An amber-colored raven was well noted.

DUMAINE

85   As upright as the cedar.

BEROWNE   *[Aside]*   Stoop, I say –

86   Her shoulder is with child.

DUMAINE   As fair as day.

BEROWNE   *[Aside]*
    Ay, as some days, but then no sun must shine.

DUMAINE
    O that I had my wish!

LONGAVILLE   *[Aside]*   And I had mine!

KING   *[Aside]*
    And I mine too, good Lord!

BEROWNE   *[Aside]*

90   Amen, so I had mine. Is not that a good word?

DUMAINE
    I would forget her, but a fever she
    Reigns in my blood and will remembered be.

BEROWNE   *[Aside]*

93   A fever in your blood? Why, then incision

94   Would let her out in saucers. Sweet misprision!

---

78 *woodcocks* (birds notable for stupidity)   82 *corporal* i.e., (1) he is an offi-cer in Cupid's army or (2) she is corporeal, human   83 *quoted* designated (i.e., her amber hair has made real amber appear foul in comparison)   84 *well noted* accurately observed (sarcasm)   85 *Stoop* stooped, misshapen   86 *is with child* i.e., has a hump   93 *incision* (for bleeding)   94 *misprision* error

DUMAINE
  Once more I'll read the ode that I have writ.
BEROWNE   *[Aside]*
  Once more I'll mark how love can vary wit.   96
    Dumaine reads his sonnet.
DUMAINE
            "On a day (alack the day!)
            Love, whose month is ever May,
            Spied a blossom passing fair
            Playing in the wanton air.   *100*
            Through the velvet leaves the wind,
            All unseen, can passage find,
            That the lover, sick to death,   103
            Wished himself the heaven's breath.
            'Air,' quoth he, 'thy cheeks may blow;
            Air, would I might triumph so,
            But, alack, my hand is sworn
            Ne'er to pluck thee from thy thorn.
            Vow, alack, for youth unmeet,   109
            Youth so apt to pluck a sweet!   *110*
            Do not call it sin in me,
            That I am forsworn for thee,
            Thou for whom great Jove would swear
            Juno but an Ethiop were;   114
            And deny himself for Jove,   115
            Turning mortal for thy love.'"
  This will I send, and something else more plain,
  That shall express my true love's fasting pain.   118
  O would the king, Berowne, and Longaville
  Were lovers too! Ill, to example ill,   120
  Would from my forehead wipe a perjured note,   121
  For none offend where all alike do dote.
LONGAVILLE   *[Advancing]*
  Dumaine, thy love is far from charity,

---

96 *vary* variegate **103** *That* so that **109** *unmeet* inappropriate **114**
Ethiop black African (racist epithet for ugliness) **115** *for* i.e., to be **118**
fasting hungering **120** *example* serve as example for **121** *note* mark

That in love's grief desir'st society.
You may look pale, but I should blush, I know,
To be o'erheard and taken napping so.

KING   *[Advancing]*
Come, sir, you blush! As his your case is such;
You chide at him, offending twice as much.
You do not love Maria! Longaville

130 Did never sonnet for her sake compile,
Nor never lay his wreathèd arms athwart
His loving bosom to keep down his heart!
I have been closely shrouded in this bush,
And marked you both, and for you both did blush.
I heard your guilty rhymes, observed your fashion,

136 Saw sighs reek from you, noted well your passion.
"Ay me!" says one; "O Jove!" the other cries;
One, her hairs were gold; crystal, the other's eyes.
   [To Longaville]
You would for paradise break faith and troth;
   [To Dumaine]

140 And Jove, for your love, would infringe an oath.
What will Berowne say when that he shall hear
Faith so infringèd, which such zeal did swear?
How will he scorn! How will he spend his wit!
How will he triumph, leap and laugh at it!
For all the wealth that ever I did see,

146 I would not have him know so much by me.

BEROWNE   *[Advancing]*
Now step I forth to whip hypocrisy.
Ah, good my liege, I pray thee pardon me.
Good heart, what grace hast thou, thus to reprove

150 These worms for loving, that art most in love?
Your eyes do make no coaches; in your tears
There is no certain princess that appears;
You'll not be perjured, 'tis a hateful thing –
Tush, none but minstrels like of sonneting!
But are you not ashamed? Nay, are you not,

---

136 *reek* breathe   **146** *by* about

All three of you, to be thus much o'ershot?   156
You found his mote; the king your mote did see;   157
But I a beam do find in each of three.   158
O what a scene of fool'ry have I seen,
Of sighs, of groans, of sorrow, and of teen!   160
O me, with what strict patience have I sat,
To see a king transformèd to a gnat;
To see great Hercules whipping a gig,   163
And profound Solomon to tune a jig,   164
And Nestor play at pushpin with the boys,   165
And critic Timon laugh at idle toys!   166
Where lies thy grief? O, tell me, good Dumaine.
And, gentle Longaville, where lies thy pain?
And where my liege's? All about the breast.
A caudle, ho!   170

KING   Too bitter is thy jest.
Are we betrayed thus to thy overview?

BEROWNE
Not you by me, but I betrayed to you;
I that am honest, I that hold it sin
To break the vow I am engagèd in,
I am betrayed by keeping company
With men like you, men of inconstancy.
When shall you see me write a thing in rhyme?
Or groan for Joan or spend a minute's time
In pruning me? When shall you hear that I   179
Will praise a hand, a foot, a face, an eye,   *180*
A gait, a state, a brow, a breast, a waist,   181
A leg, a limb —

KING   Soft! Whither away so fast?
A true man or a thief, that gallops so?   183

---

156 *o'ershot* worsted   **157** *You* (Longaville); *his* (Dumaine's); *your* (Longaville's)   **157, 158** *mote, beam* i.e., small defect, large defect (cf. Matthew 7:3–5; Luke 6:41–42)   **160** *teen* grief   **163** *gig* top   **164** *tune* play   **165** *Nestor* the oldest and most reverend of the Greek chieftains; *pushpin* a child's game   **166** *critic* cynic; *Timon* Greek misanthrope; *laugh . . . toys* i.e., delight in useless trifles   **170** *caudle* warm liquid nourishment for the ill   **179** *pruning* trimming, barbering   **181** *state* bearing   **183** *true* honest

BEROWNE

184   I post from love. Good lover, let me go.

     Enter Jaquenetta [with a letter] and [Costard the]
     Clown.

JAQUENETTA

    God bless the king!

KING   What present hast thou there?

COSTARD

186   Some certain treason.

KING   What makes treason here?

COSTARD

    Nay, it makes nothing, sir.

KING   If it mar nothing neither,

    The treason and you go in peace away together.

JAQUENETTA

    I beseech your grace let this letter be read:

190   Our person misdoubts it; 'twas treason, he said.

KING   Berowne, read it over.

     [Berowne] reads the letter.

    Where hadst thou it?

JAQUENETTA   Of Costard.

KING   Where hadst thou it?

COSTARD   Of Dun Adramadio, Dun Adramadio.

     [Berowne tears the letter.]

KING

    How now, what is in you? Why dost thou tear it?

BEROWNE

197   A toy, my liege, a toy. Your grace needs not fear it.

LONGAVILLE

    It did move him to passion, and therefore let's hear it.

DUMAINE   *[Picking up the pieces]*

    It is Berowne's writing, and here is his name.

BEROWNE   *[To Costard]*

200   Ah, you whoreson loggerhead, you were born to do me
      shame.

----

184 *post* ride fast **186** *makes* does **190** *person* parson; *misdoubts* suspects
197 *toy* trifle **200** *loggerhead* blockhead

Guilty, my lord, guilty. I confess, I confess.

KING   What?

BEROWNE

That you three fools lacked me fool to make up the   203
  mess.
He, he, and you – e'en you, my liege, and I,
Are pickpurses in love, and we deserve to die.   205
O, dismiss this audience, and I shall tell you more.

DUMAINE

Now the number is even.

BEROWNE   True, true; we are four.
Will these turtles be gone?   208

KING   Hence, sirs, away.

COSTARD

Walk aside the true folk, and let the traitors stay.
                    [Exeunt Costard and Jaquenetta.]

BEROWNE

Sweet lords, sweet lovers, O, let us embrace!   210
  As true we are as flesh and blood can be.
The sea will ebb and flow, heaven show his face.
  Young blood doth not obey an old decree.
We cannot cross the cause why we were born;   214
Therefore, of all hands must we be forsworn.   215

KING

What, did these rent lines show some love of thine?   216

BEROWNE

Did they? quoth you. Who sees the heavenly Rosaline,
That, like a rude and savage man of Inde,   218
  At the first opening of the gorgeous east,
Bows not his vassal head and, strucken blind,   220
  Kisses the base ground with obedient breast?
What peremptory eagle-sighted eye   222
  Dares look upon the heaven of her brow,

---

203 *mess* a group of four at table   205 *pickpurses* i.e., cheaters   208 *turtles*
turtledoves, lovers   214 *cross . . . born* combat the cause of our birth (love
between the sexes)   215 *of all hands* in all events, inevitably   216 *rent lines*
torn verses   218 *rude* ignorant; *Inde* India   222 *peremptory* bold; *eagle-
sighted* (the eagle was held to be the only bird able to look directly at the sun)

That is not blinded by her majesty?

KING

What zeal, what fury, hath inspired thee now?

My love, her mistress, is a gracious moon,

227   She, an attending star, scarce seen a light.

BEROWNE

My eyes are then no eyes, nor I Berowne.

O, but for my love, day would turn to night!

230   Of all complexions the culled sovereignty

Do meet, as at a fair, in her fair cheek,

232   Where several worthies make one dignity,

233   Where nothing wants that want itself doth seek.

234   Lend me the flourish of all gentle tongues –

235   Fie, painted rhetoric! O, she needs it not.

236   To things of sale a seller's praise belongs.

She passes praise – then praise too short doth blot.

A withered hermit, fivescore winters worn,

Might shake off fifty, looking in her eye.

240   Beauty doth varnish age as if new-born,

And gives the crutch the cradle's infancy.

O, 'tis the sun that maketh all things shine!

KING

By heaven, thy love is black as ebony.

BEROWNE

244   Is ebony like her? O word divine!

A wife of such wood were felicity.

246   O, who can give an oath? Where is a book,

That I may swear beauty doth beauty lack,

248   If that she learn not of her eye to look?

No face is fair that is not full so black.

KING

250   O paradox! Black is the badge of hell,

---

227 *scarce . . . light* a hardly visible light   230 *the culled sovereignty* those selected as best   232 *several worthies* various excellences   233 *wants* lacks; *want* desire   234 *flourish* adornment   235 *painted* artificial   236 *of sale* for sale   244 *word* (often emended to "wood")   246 *book* i.e., Bible   248 *of . . . look* i.e., from her (dark) eyes how to appear

The hue of dungeons, and the school of night,   251
And beauty's crest becomes the heavens well.   252
BEROWNE
Devils soonest tempt, resembling spirits of light.   253
O, if in black my lady's brows be decked,
   It mourns that painting and usurping hair   255
Should ravish doters with a false aspect,
   And therefore is she born to make black fair.
Her favor turns the fashion of the days,   258
   For native blood is counted painting now;   259
And therefore red that would avoid dispraise   260
   Paints itself black to imitate her brow.
DUMAINE
To look like her are chimney sweepers black.
LONGAVILLE
   And since her time are colliers counted bright.   263
KING
   And Ethiops of their sweet complexion crack.   264
DUMAINE
   Dark needs no candles now, for dark is light.
BEROWNE
Your mistresses dare never come in rain,
   For fear their colors should be washed away.   267
KING
'Twere good yours did, for, sir, to tell you plain,
   I'll find a fairer face not washed today.   269
BEROWNE
I'll prove her fair, or talk till doomsday here.   270
KING
   No devil will fright thee then so much as she.   271

---

251 *school of night* (the school where night learns how to be really dark)
252 *beauty's crest* (the sun, not blackness)   253 *resembling* simulating   255
usurping false   258 *favor* face   259 *native blood* i.e., naturally red cheeks;
counted accounted   263 *colliers* coal sellers   264 *crack* boast   267 (1) because their pale color is almost washed away already, (2) because their color is
produced by cosmetics   269 *I'll . . . today* i.e., there are unwashed faces
fairer than hers   271 *then* i.e., on doomsday

DUMAINE
  I never knew man hold vile stuff so dear.
LONGAVILLE
  Look, here's thy love –
  [Shows his shoe.]   my foot and her face see.
BEROWNE
  O, if the streets were pavèd with thine eyes,
    Her feet were much too dainty for such tread.
DUMAINE
276 O vile! Then, as she goes, what upward lies
    The street should see as she walked overhead.
KING
  But what of this? Are we not all in love?
BEROWNE
    Nothing so sure, and thereby all forsworn.
KING
280 Then leave this chat, and, good Berowne, now prove
    Our loving lawful and our faith not torn.
DUMAINE
282 Ay, marry, there; some flattery for this evil.
LONGAVILLE
  O some authority how to proceed,
284 Some tricks, some quillets, how to cheat the devil.
DUMAINE
  Some salve for perjury.
BEROWNE   'Tis more than need.
286 Have at you, then, affection's men-at-arms!
  Consider what you first did swear unto:
  To fast, to study, and to see no woman –
  Flat treason 'gainst the kingly state of youth.
290 Say, can you fast? Your stomachs are too young,
  And abstinence engenders maladies.
291.1   [And where that you have vowed to study, lords,

---

276 *what upward lies* (her genitals) 282 *flattery* i.e., soothing lies 284 *quillets* quibbles 286 *affection's men-at-arms* passion's followers 291.1–291.23 *And where . . . learning there* (This passage is clearly a first draft, printed in error, for the passage that follows.) 291.1 *where that* whereas

In that each of you have forsworn his book,   291.2
Can you still dream and pore and thereon look?
For when would you, my lord, or you, or you,
Have found the ground of study's excellence   291.5
Without the beauty of a woman's face?
From women's eyes this doctrine I derive:
They are the ground, the books, the academes,   291.8
From whence doth spring the true Promethean fire.   291.9
Why, universal plodding poisons up   *291.10*
The nimble spirits in the arteries,
As motion and long-during action tires   291.12
The sinewy vigor of the traveler.
Now, for not looking on a woman's face,
You have in that forsworn the use of eyes,
And study too, the causer of your vow;
For where is any author in the world
Teaches such beauty as a woman's eye?
Learning is but an adjunct to ourself,
And where we are our learning likewise is.   *291.20*
Then when ourselves we see in ladies' eyes,
With ourselves,
Do we not likewise see our learning there?]
O, we have made a vow to study, lords,
And in that vow we have forsworn our books;   293
For when would you, my liege, or you, or you,
In leaden contemplation have found out
Such fiery numbers as the prompting eyes   296
Of beauty's tutors have enriched you with?
Other slow arts entirely keep the brain,   298
And therefore, finding barren practicers,
Scarce show a harvest of their heavy toil;   *300*
But love, first learnèd in a lady's eyes,
Lives not alone immurèd in the brain,   302

291.2 *In that* inasmuch as; *book* i.e., a woman's face   291.5 *ground* basis
291.8 *academes* academies   291.9 *Promethean* divine (the god Prometheus
brought fire from heaven to earth)   291.12 *long-during* enduring   293
books i.e., women's faces   296 *numbers* verses, poems   298 *arts* branches of
knowledge; *keep* remain in   302 *alone immurèd* only shut up

303   But, with the motion of all elements,
       Courses as swift as thought in every power,
       And gives to every power a double power,
306   Above their functions and their offices.
       It adds a precious seeing to the eye:
308   A lover's eyes will gaze an eagle blind.
       A lover's ear will hear the lowest sound,
310   When the suspicious head of theft is stopped.
311   Love's feeling is more soft and sensible
312   Than are the tender horns of cockled snails.
313   Love's tongue proves dainty Bacchus gross in taste.
       For valor, is not Love a Hercules,
315   Still climbing trees in the Hesperides?
316   Subtle as Sphinx, as sweet and musical
       As bright Apollo's lute, strung with his hair.
       And when Love speaks, the voice of all the gods
       Make heaven drowsy with the harmony.
320   Never durst poet touch a pen to write
321   Until his ink were tempered with Love's sighs.
       O, then his lines would ravish savage ears
       And plant in tyrants mild humility.
       From women's eyes this doctrine I derive.
325   They sparkle still the right Promethean fire;
       They are the books, the arts, the academes,
       That show, contain, and nourish all the world,
       Else none at all in aught proves excellent.
       Then fools you were these women to forswear,
330   Or, keeping what is sworn, you will prove fools.

---

303 *elements* (fire, air, water, earth, each of which had its own proper motion
and proper seat in the body as elsewhere) **306** *Above their functions* i.e., beyond their ordinary functions **308** *A lover's . . . blind* (cf. IV.3.222) **310**
When . . . stopped i.e., when even a timorously alert thief hears nothing **311**
sensible sensitive **312** *cockled* in shells **313** *Bacchus* god of wine and feast-
ing **315** *Hesperides* (where the golden apples grew that Hercules had to pick
in one of his labors) **316** *Sphinx* Greek mythical monster who killed
passersby who failed to solve her riddle **321** *tempered* cooled and refined
325 *Promethean* divine (see 291.9) **330** *what is sworn* i.e., the oaths

For wisdom's sake, a word that all men love,
Or for love's sake, a word that loves all men,   332
Or for men's sake, the authors of these women,
Or women's sake, by whom we men are men,
Let us once lose our oaths to find ourselves,   335
Or else we lose ourselves to keep our oaths.
It is religion to be thus forsworn,
For charity itself fulfills the law   338
And who can sever love from charity?

KING
Saint Cupid then! And, soldiers, to the field!   *340*

BEROWNE
Advance your standards, and upon them, lords!   341
Pell-mell, down with them! But be first advised,
In conflict that you get the sun of them.   343

LONGAVILLE
Now to plain dealing – lay these glozes by –   344
Shall we resolve to woo these girls of France?

KING
And win them too. Therefore let us devise
Some entertainment for them in their tents.

BEROWNE
First from the park let us conduct them thither;
Then homeward every man attach the hand   349
Of his fair mistress. In the afternoon   *350*
We will with some strange pastime solace them,
Such as the shortness of the time can shape,
For revels, dances, masques, and merry hours
Forerun fair Love, strewing her way with flowers.   354

KING
Away, away! No time shall be omitted

---

332 *loves* i.e., is lovable to   335 *once* for once, at once (Berowne parodies
Matthew 16:25)   338 *For . . . law* (Romans 13:8: ". . . for he that loveth another hath fulfilled the law")   341 *standards* (punning on "standers," "erec-
tions")   343 *get . . . them* i.e., maneuver them into facing the sun (with play
on "beget son")   344 *glozes* sophistries   349 *attach* seize   354 *Forerun* run
before

356   That will be time, and may by us be fitted.

BEROWNE

357   *Allons! allons!* Sowed cockle reaped no corn,
     And justice always whirls in equal measure.
     Light wenches may prove plagues to men forsworn;
360   If so, our copper buys no better treasure.

                            [Exeunt.]

                *

   ❧ **V.1**   *Enter [Holofernes] the Pedant, [Nathaniel] the Curate, and Dull [the Constable].*

1   HOLOFERNES   *Satis quid sufficit.*
2   NATHANIEL   I praise God for you, sir. Your reasons at dinner have been sharp and sententious, pleasant with-
4   out scurrility, witty without affection, audacious with-
5   out impudency, learned without opinion, and strange without heresy. I did converse this *quondam* day with a companion of the king's, who is intituled, nominated, or called, Don Adriano de Armado.
9   HOLOFERNES   *Novi hominum tanquam te.* His humor is
10   lofty, his discourse peremptory, his tongue filed, his eye ambitious, his gait majestical, and his general behavior
12   vain, ridiculous, and thrasonical. He is too picked, too
13   spruce, too affected, too odd, as it were, too peregrinate, as I may call it.
15   NATHANIEL   A most singular and choice epithet.
     Draw out his table book.

---

356 *be time* be long enough; *fitted* utilized   357 *Allons* let's go (French); *cockle* a variety of weed; *corn* wheat   360 *copper* base coin (i.e., as men forsworn, they have little of worth to offer)
     V.1   1 *Satis quid sufficit* (misquotation of *satis est quod sufficit:* enough is as good as a feast – they have just had dinner)   2 *reasons* discourses   4 *affection* affectation   5 *opinion* arrogance; *strange* novel   9 *Novi . . . te* I know the man as well as I know you   10 *tongue filed* language refined   12 *thrasonical* boastful; *picked* finicking   13 *peregrinate* exotic   15 *singular* unique; **s.d.** *table book* notebook

HOLOFERNES   He draweth out the thread of his verbosity
finer than the staple of his argument. I abhor such fa-   17
natical phantasims, such insociable and point-devise   18
companions, such rackers of orthography as to speak
"dout" *sine* "b" when he should say "doubt"; "det"   20
when he should pronounce "debt" – d, e, b, t, not d, e, t.
He clepeth a calf "cauf"; half "hauf"; neighbor *vocatur*   22
"nebor," neigh abbreviated "ne." This is abhominable,
which he would call "abominable." It insinuateth me of
insanire. Ne intelligis, domine? To make frantic, lunatic.   25
NATHANIEL   *Laus Deo bone intelligo.*   26
HOLOFERNES   *Bone? Bone* for *bene!* Priscian a little   27
scratched – 'twill serve.   28

 Enter [Armado the] Braggart, [Moth the] Boy [, and
 Costard the Clown].

NATHANIEL   *Videsne quis venit?*   29
HOLOFERNES   *Video, et gaudeo.*   30
ARMADO   *[To Moth]* Chirrah!
HOLOFERNES   *Quare* "chirrah," not "sirrah"?   32
ARMADO   Men of peace, well encountered.
HOLOFERNES   Most military sir, salutation.
MOTH   *[Aside to Costard]* They have been at a great feast
of languages and stolen the scraps.
COSTARD   O, they have lived long on the alms basket of   37
words. I marvel thy master hath not eaten thee for a
word, for thou art not so long by the head as *honorific-*   39

---

17 *staple* fiber; *argument* subject matter   18 *phantasims* (cf. IV.1.100); *insociable* incompatible; *point-devise* precise   20 *sine* without   22 *clepeth* calls;
vocatur is called   25 *insanire* madness; *Ne . . . domine* do you understand, sir
26 *Laus . . . intelligo* praise God, I understand well   27 *Priscian* i.e., Latin
grammar (after the fifth-century grammarian whose textbooks were long
standard)   28 *scratched* marred   29 *Videsne quis venit* do you see who comes
30 *Video, et gaudeo* I see and rejoice   32 *Quare* why   37 *alms basket* container in which scraps for the poor were gathered   39 *word* (punning on
Moth's name as French *mot,* "word")   39–40 *honorificabilitudinitatibus*
condition of being capable of honors (given in the dative plural and often
cited as the "longest word" in existence)

40 *abilitudinitatibus.* Thou art easier swallowed than a
41 flapdragon.

42 MOTH Peace! The peal begins.

43 ARMADO Monsieur, are you not lettered?

44 MOTH Yes, yes! He teaches boys the hornbook. What is
a, b, spelled backward with the horn on his head?

46 HOLOFERNES Ba, *pueritia,* with a horn added.

MOTH Ba, most silly sheep with a horn. You hear his
learning.

49 HOLOFERNES *Quis, quis,* thou consonant?

50 MOTH The last of the five vowels, if you repeat them; or
the fifth, if I.

HOLOFERNES I will repeat them: a, e, i –

53 MOTH The sheep. The other two concludes it – o, u.

ARMADO Now, by the salt wave of the *Mediterraneum,* a
55 sweet touch, a quick venue of wit! Snip, snap, quick
and home! It rejoiceth my intellect. True wit!

57 MOTH Offered by a child to an old man – which is wit-
old.

59 HOLOFERNES What is the figure? What is the figure?

60 MOTH Horns.

HOLOFERNES Thou disputes like an infant. Go whip thy
62 gig.

MOTH Lend me your horn to make one, and I will whip
64 about your infamy *manu cita.* A gig of a cuckold's horn.

COSTARD An I had but one penny in the world, thou
shouldst have it to buy gingerbread. Hold, there is the
67 very remuneration I had of thy master, thou halfpenny
purse of wit, thou pigeon egg of discretion. O, an the

---

41 *flapdragon* a drink of brandy containing a burning raisin **42** *peal* i.e.,
clatter of tongues **43** *lettered* i.e., a man of letters **44** *hornbook* printed
sheets covered by transparent horn, for teaching the alphabet **46** *pueritia*
child **49** *Quis* what; *consonant* i.e., nonentity (because in pronunciation the
consonants require vowels) **50** *last* i.e., u, "you," "ewe" **53** *o, u* (oh you)
55 *venue* sally **57–58** *wit-old* i.e., wittol, tame cuckold **59** *figure* metaphor
62 *gig* top **64** *manu cita* with ready hand (the Latin is a conjectural emendation for the meaningless "unum cita" of the quarto) **67–68** *halfpenny
purse* (a novelty purse, just large enough to hold a halfpenny)

heavens were so pleased that thou wert but my bastard,
what a joyful father wouldest thou make me! Go to,   70
thou hast it *ad* dunghill, at the fingers' ends, as they say.   71
HOLOFERNES   O, I smell false Latin! "Dunghill" for
unguem.
ARMADO   Arts man, *preambulate.* We will be singued   74
from the barbarous. Do you not educate youth at the
chargehouse on the top of the mountain?   76
HOLOFERNES   Or *mons,* the hill.
ARMADO   At your sweet pleasure, for the mountain.
HOLOFERNES   I do, *sans question.*   79
ARMADO   Sir, it is the king's most sweet pleasure and af- 80
fection to congratulate the princess at her pavilion in   81
the posteriors of this day, which the rude multitude call
the afternoon.
HOLOFERNES   The posterior of the day, most generous   84
sir, is liable, congruent, and measurable for the after-   85
noon. The word is well culled, chose, sweet and apt, I
do assure you, sir, I do assure.
ARMADO   Sir, the king is a noble gentleman, and my
familiar, I do assure ye, very good friend. For what is   89
inward between us, let it pass. I do beseech thee re-   90
member thy courtesy. I beseech thee apparel thy head.   91
And among other importunate and most serious designs, and of great import indeed, too – but let that
pass, for I must tell thee, it will please his grace, by the
world, sometime to lean upon my poor shoulder, and
with his royal finger thus dally with my excrement,   96
with my mustachio – but, sweet heart, let that pass. By

---

71 *ad dunghill* (malapropism for *ad unguem* – i.e., on the nail)   74 *Arts man*
scholar; *preambulate* come (in italics in Q as a foreign word); *singued* distinguished   76–78 *chargehouse . . . mountain* (an obscure allusion, possibly involving an academic joke about the kind of school mentioned in Erasmus's
Familiaria colloquia, where the paying pupils acquired more lice than Latin)
79 *sans* without   81 *congratulate* greet   84 *generous* cultivated   85 *liable*
suitable; *congruent* appropriate; *measurable* meet   89 *familiar* intimate   90
inward private   91 *thy courtesy* i.e., that you have removed your hat   96 *excrement* excrescence, hair

the world, I recount no fable: some certain special honors it pleaseth his greatness to impart to Armado, a sol-
100   dier, a man of travel, that hath seen the world – but let
that pass. The very all of all is (but, sweet heart, I do
implore secrecy) that the king would have me present
the princess, sweet chuck, with some delightful osten-
104   tation, or show, or pageant, or antic, or firework. Now,
understanding that the curate and your sweet self are
good at such eruptions and sudden breaking-out of
mirth, as it were, I have acquainted you withal, to the
end to crave your assistance.

109   HOLOFERNES   Sir, you shall present before her the Nine
110   Worthies. Sir Nathaniel, as concerning some entertainment of time, some show in the posterior of this day, to
be rendered by our assistance, the king's command, and
this most gallant, illustrate, and learned gentleman, before the princess – I say, none so fit as to present the
Nine Worthies.

NATHANIEL   Where will you find men worthy enough to
present them?

118   HOLOFERNES   Joshua, yourself; myself Judas Maccabaeus;
and this gallant gentleman, Hector; this swain, because
120   of his great limb or joint, shall pass Pompey the Great;
the page, Hercules –

ARMADO   Pardon, sir – error. He is not quantity enough
for that Worthy's thumb, he is not so big as the end of
his club.

---

104 *antic* a pageant in grotesque costume   109–110 *Nine Worthies* con-
querors commonly featured in folk drama and pageants: Hector of Troy,
Alexander the Great, Julius Caesar, Joshua, David, Judas Maccabaeus, King
Arthur, Charlemagne, and Godfrey of Bouillon – making up three virtuous
pagans, three Jewish heroes, and three Christian warriors; in the present case
Hercules and Pompey are substituted for more usual figures   118 *Joshua,
yourself* (though Nathaniel plays Alexander)   118–19 *myself . . . Hector* (Q
gives no role to Holofernes and Judas to Armado; the emendation adopted
here is plausible, though Shakespeare may not have sorted out the casting
properly)   120 *pass* perform

HOLOFERNES   Shall I have audience? He shall present Her-   125
cules in minority. His enter and exit shall be strangling a   126
snake; and I will have an apology for that purpose.   127

MOTH   An excellent device! So if any of the audience
hiss, you may cry, "Well done, Hercules! Now thou
crushest the snake!" That is the way to make an offense   130
gracious, though few have the grace to do it.

ARMADO   For the rest of the Worthies?

HOLOFERNES   I will play three myself.

MOTH   Thrice-worthy gentleman!

ARMADO   Shall I tell you a thing?

HOLOFERNES   We attend.

ARMADO   We will have, if this fadge not, an antic. I be-   137
seech you, follow.

HOLOFERNES   *Via,* goodman Dull! Thou hast spoken no   139
word all this while.   140

DULL   Nor understood none neither, sir.

HOLOFERNES   *Allons!* we will employ thee.   142

DULL   I'll make one in a dance, or so, or I will play on
the tabor to the Worthies, and let them dance the hay.   144

HOLOFERNES   Most dull, honest Dull. To our sport, away!
                                          Exeunt.

*

❧ **V.2** *Enter the Ladies [Princess, Katherine, Rosaline,
and Maria].*

PRINCESS
Sweet hearts, we shall be rich ere we depart
If fairings come thus plentifully in.   2

---

125 *audience* a hearing   126 *in minority* as a child   127 *snake* (the legendary Hercules strangled in his cradle two snakes sent by Juno to destroy
him); *apology* explanation, justification   137 *fadge not* does not succeed;
antic (cf. l. 104)   139 *Via* i.e., go on (a cry of encouragement)   142 *Allons*
let's go (French)   144 *tabor* small drum; *the hay* a country dance resembling
a reel
   V.2 2 *fairings* gifts, tokens bought at a fair

3   A lady walled about with diamonds!
    Look you what I have from the loving king.
ROSALINE
    Madam, came nothing else along with that?
PRINCESS
    Nothing but this? Yes, as much love in rhyme
    As would be crammed up in a sheet of paper,
    Writ o' both sides the leaf, margin and all,
9   That he was fain to seal on Cupid's name.
ROSALINE
10 That was the way to make his godhead wax,
    For he hath been five thousand year a boy.
KATHERINE
12 Ay, and a shrewd unhappy gallows too.
ROSALINE
13 You'll ne'er be friends with him: a killed your sister.
KATHERINE
    He made her melancholy, sad, and heavy,
15 And so she died. Had she been light, like you,
    Of such a merry, nimble, stirring spirit,
    She might ha' been a grandam ere she died,
    And so may you, for a light heart lives long.
ROSALINE
19 What's your dark meaning, mouse, of this light word?
KATHERINE
20 A light condition in a beauty dark.
ROSALINE
    We need more light to find your meaning out.
KATHERINE
22 You'll mar the light by taking it in snuff;
23 Therefore, I'll darkly end the argument.

---

3 (the picture on the diamond pendant or brooch she has been given)
9 *That . . . name* i.e., so that he had to put his seal over where he had written
"Cupid"   10 *wax* grow (with play on "wax seal")   12 *shrewd unhappy gal-*
lows vexing mischievous knave   13 *a* he   15 *light* cheerful   19 *light* frivo-
lous   20 *light* wanton, wayward   22 *taking . . . snuff* i.e., being offended by
it (with play on "snuffing a candle")   23 *darkly* without clarifying

ROSALINE
   Look, what you do, you do it still i' th' dark.   24
KATHERINE
   So do not you, for you are a light wench.
ROSALINE
   Indeed I weigh not you, and therefore light.   26
KATHERINE
   You weigh me not? O, that's you care not for me.
ROSALINE
   Great reason, for past cure is still past care.   28
PRINCESS
   Well bandied both, a set of wit well played.   29
   But, Rosaline, you have a favor too: 30
   Who sent it? and what is it?
ROSALINE   I would you knew.
   An if my face were but as fair as yours,
   My favor were as great. Be witness this.
   Nay, I have verses too, I thank Berowne,
   The numbers true, and, were the numb'ring too,   35
   I were the fairest goddess on the ground.
   I am compared to twenty thousand fairs.   37
   O, he hath drawn my picture in his letter!
PRINCESS   Anything like?
ROSALINE   Much in the letters, nothing in the praise.   40
PRINCESS   Beauteous as ink – a good conclusion.
KATHERINE   Fair as a text B in a copybook.   42
ROSALINE
   'Ware pencils, ho! Let me not die your debtor,   43
   My red dominical, my golden letter.   44

---

24 *do* (punning on "have sex")   26 *weigh* (1) equal in weight, (2) regard   28 *past cure* (Rosaline is calling Katherine "incurable")   29 *bandied* volleyed   30 *favor* gift   35 *numbers* meter; *numb'ring* reckoning, valuing   37 *fairs* fair women   40 *letters . . . praise* i.e., in the orthography rather than in the content   42 *a text B* a capital printed in Gothic text or "black-letter" (the allusion is to Rosaline's dark complexion)   43 *'Ware pencils* i.e., have at you (with the metaphor still drawn from the arts of writing and portraiture)   44 *red dominical* the red letter S used to mark Sundays in almanacs, etc. (alluding to Katherine's ruddy complexion); *golden letter* (also used to mark Sundays, alluding to her "amber hairs," IV.3.83)

45   O, that your face were not so full of O's!
PRINCESS
46   A pox of that jest, and I beshrew all shrews!
        But, Katherine, what was sent to you from fair Du-
            maine?
KATHERINE
        Madam, this glove.
PRINCESS   Did he not send you twain?
KATHERINE
        Yes, madam; and moreover,
50   Some thousand verses of a faithful lover:
51   A huge translation of hypocrisy,
52   Vilely compiled, profound simplicity.
MARIA
        This, and these pearls, to me sent Longaville.
        The letter is too long by half a mile.
PRINCESS
        I think no less. Dost thou not wish in heart
        The chain were longer and the letter short?
MARIA
57   Ay, or I would these hands might never part.
PRINCESS
        We are wise girls to mock our lovers so.
ROSALINE
59   They are worse fools to purchase mocking so.
60   That same Berowne I'll torture ere I go.
61   O that I knew he were but in by th' week!
        How I would make him fawn, and beg, and seek,
        And wait the season, and observe the times,
        And spend his prodigal wits in bootless rhymes,
65   And shape his service wholly to my hests,

---

45 O's (Rosaline hints that Katherine's face is scarred by smallpox and hence
she needs cosmetic "pencils" to cover the marks) 46 *A pox* (commenting on
Rosaline's joke and rebuking her for it); *beshrew all shrews* curse all scolds
51 *translation* rendition 52 *simplicity* stupidity 57 (she has wrapped the
chain around her hands) 59 *purchase* i.e., bid for, invite 61 *in . . . week*
permanently caught 65 *hests* behests, commands

And make him proud to make me proud that jests!   66
So pertaunt-like would I o'ersway his state   67
That he should be my fool, and I his fate.   68

PRINCESS
None are so surely caught, when they are catched,
As wit turned fool. Folly, in wisdom hatched,   70
Hath wisdom's warrant and the help of school
And wit's own grace to grace a learnèd fool.

ROSALINE
The blood of youth burns not with such excess
As gravity's revolt to wantonness.

MARIA
Folly in fools bears not so strong a note
As fool'ry in the wise when wit doth dote,   76
Since all the power thereof it doth apply
To prove, by wit, worth in simplicity.
     Enter Boyet.

PRINCESS
Here comes Boyet, and mirth is in his face.

BOYET
O, I am stabbed with laughter! Where's her grace?   80

PRINCESS
Thy news, Boyet?

BOYET   Prepare, madam, prepare!
Arm, wenches, arm! Encounters mounted are
Against your peace. Love doth approach disguised,
Armèd in arguments; you'll be surprised.   84
Muster your wits, stand in your own defense,
Or hide your heads like cowards, and fly hence.

PRINCESS
Saint Denis to Saint Cupid! What are they   87
That charge their breath against us? Say, scout, say.

---

66 *proud to . . . jests* i.e., take pride in being the victim of my mockery 67
pertaunt pair-taunt (winning hand in a card game called post and pair) 68
fool plaything 76 *dote* grow foolish 84 *surprised* i.e., overcome by surprise
attack 87 *Saint Denis* patron saint of France

BOYET
> Under the cool shade of a sycamore
90 > I thought to close mine eyes some half an hour,
> When, lo, to interrupt my purposed rest,
92 > Toward that shade I might behold addressed
> The king and his companions! Warily
> I stole into a neighbor thicket by,
> And overheard what you shall overhear –
> That, by and by, disguised they will be here.
> Their herald is a pretty knavish page,
98 > That well by heart hath conned his embassage.
99 > Action and accent did they teach him there:
100 > "Thus must thou speak, and thus thy body bear."
101 > And ever and anon they made a doubt
> Presence majestical would put him out,
> "For," quoth the king, "an angel shalt thou see,
104 > Yet fear not thou, but speak audaciously."
> The boy replied, "An angel is not evil;
> I should have feared her had she been a devil."
> With that all laughed and clapped him on the shoulder,
> Making the bold wag by their praises bolder.
109 > One rubbed his elbows thus, and fleered, and swore
110 > A better speech was never spoke before.
111 > Another, with his finger and his thumb,
112 > Cried "*Via*, we will do't, come what will come!"
> The third he capered and cried, "All goes well!"
114 > The fourth turned on the toe, and down he fell.
> With that they all did tumble on the ground
116 > With such a zealous laughter, so profound,
117 > That in this spleen ridiculous appears,
> To check their folly, passion's solemn tears.

PRINCESS
> But what, but what? Come they to visit us?

---

92 *addressed* marching   98 *conned* learned; *embassage* message of state   99
Action gesture   101 *made a doubt* expressed a fear   104 *audaciously* boldly
109 *fleered* grinned   111 *with . . . thumb* i.e., with a snapping of the fingers
112 *Via* go on   114 *turned . . . toe* pirouetted   116 *profound* deep   117
spleen ridiculous fit of laughing

BOYET

> They do, they do; and are appareled thus,   *120*
> Like Muscovites or Russians, as I guess.   121
> Their purpose is to parley, to court and dance;
> And every one his love suit will advance
> Unto his several mistress, which they'll know   124
> By favors several which they did bestow.

PRINCESS

> And will they so? The gallants shall be tasked,   126
> For, ladies, we will every one be masked,
> And not a man of them shall have the grace,   128
> Despite of suit, to see a lady's face.   129
> Hold, Rosaline, this favor thou shalt wear,   130
> And then the king will court thee for his dear.
> Hold, take thou this, my sweet, and give me thine,
> So shall Berowne take me for Rosaline.
>   *[She changes favors with Rosaline.]*
> And change you favors too, so shall your loves
> Woo contrary, deceived by these removes.   135
>   *[Maria and Katherine change favors.]*

ROSALINE

> Come on, then – wear the favors most in sight.   136

KATHERINE

> But in this changing what is your intent?

PRINCESS

> The effect of my intent is to cross theirs.
> They do it but in mockery merriment,   139
> And mock for mock is only my intent.   *140*
> Their several counsels they unbosom shall   141
> To loves mistook and so be mocked withal
> Upon the next occasion that we meet,
> With visages displayed, to talk and greet.

---

121 (a line, rhyming with "guess," has probably been lost)   **124** *which*
whom   **126** *tasked* hard put to it   **128** *grace* favor   **129** *Despite of suit* in
spite of his plea   **130–31** (these lines are sometimes assumed to be a draft
for 132–33, but they balance the exchange)   **135** *removes* exchanges   **136**
most in sight conspicuously   **139** *mockery* mocking   **141** *several* individual;
unbosom confide

ROSALINE
   But shall we dance if they desire us to't?
PRINCESS
146   No, to the death we will not move a foot,
   Nor to their penned speech render we no grace,
   But while 'tis spoke each turn away her face.
BOYET
   Why, that contempt will kill the speaker's heart,
150   And quite divorce his memory from his part.
PRINCESS
   Therefore I do it, and I make no doubt
   The rest will ne'er come in if he be out.
   There's no such sport as sport by sport o'erthrown,
154   To make theirs ours, and ours none but our own.
155   So shall we stay, mocking intended game,
   And they, well mocked, depart away with shame.
      Sound Trumpets.
BOYET
157   The trumpet sounds. Be masked. The maskers come.
      [The Ladies mask.]
      Enter Blackamoors with music; [Moth] the Boy, with a
      speech, and the [King and his] Lords disguised.
MOTH
   "All hail, the richest beauties on the earth!"
BOYET
159   Beauties no richer than rich taffeta.
MOTH
160   "A holy parcel of the fairest dames,"
      The Ladies turn their backs to him.
   "That ever turned their – backs – to mortal views!"
BEROWNE   "Their eyes," villain, "their eyes."
MOTH
   "That ever turned their eyes to mortal views!
   Out –"

---

146 *No . . . death* i.e., not on your life   154 *theirs* i.e., their sport   155 *game*
i.e., mockery   157 **s.d.** *Blackamoors . . . music* musicians dressed as black
Africans   159 *taffeta* i.e., the cloth of their masks

BOYET   True. "Out" indeed.   165

MOTH
  "Out of your favors, heavenly spirits, vouchsafe
  Not to behold –"

BEROWNE   "Once to behold," rogue.

MOTH
  "Once to behold with your sun-beamèd eyes,
  – with your sun-beamèd eyes –"   170

BOYET
  They will not answer to that epithet.
  You were best call it "daughter-beamèd eyes."   172

MOTH
  They do not mark me, and that brings me out.

BEROWNE
  Is this your perfectness? Be gone, you rogue!

                                        [Exit Moth.]

ROSALINE   *[As the Princess]*
  What would these strangers? Know their minds, Boyet.   175
  If they do speak our language, 'tis our will
  That some plain man recount their purposes.
  Know what they would.

BOYET
  What would you with the princess?

BEROWNE
  Nothing but peace and gentle visitation.   180

ROSALINE
  What would they, say they?

BOYET
  Nothing but peace and gentle visitation.

ROSALINE
  Why, that they have, and bid them so be gone.

BOYET
  She says you have it and you may be gone.

---

165 *Out* i.e., out of his part   172 *daughter* (the inevitable play on "sun-son")
175 (from here to line 266 Rosaline plays the princess)

KING

185   Say to her, we have measured many miles,

186   To tread a measure with her on this grass.

BOYET

    They say that they have measured many a mile,

    To tread a measure with you on this grass.

ROSALINE

    It is not so. Ask them how many inches

190   Is in one mile. If they have measured many,

    The measure then of one is easily told.

BOYET

    If to come hither you have measured miles,

    And many miles, the princess bids you tell

    How many inches doth fill up one mile.

BEROWNE

    Tell her we measure them by weary steps.

BOYET

    She hears herself.

ROSALINE   How many weary steps,

    Of many weary miles you have o'ergone,

    Are numbered in the travel of one mile?

BEROWNE

    We number nothing that we spend for you.

200   Our duty is so rich, so infinite,

    That we may do it still without account.

    Vouchsafe to show the sunshine of your face,

    That we, like savages, may worship it.

ROSALINE

    My face is but a moon, and clouded too.

KING

    Blessèd are clouds, to do as such clouds do.

    Vouchsafe, bright moon, and these thy stars, to shine

207   (Those clouds removed) upon our watery eyne.

ROSALINE

    O vain petitioner, beg a greater matter!

----

185 *measured* paced   **186** *measure* dance   **207** *eyne* eyes

Thou now requests but moonshine in the water.   209

KING

Then in our measure do but vouchsafe one change.   210

Thou bid'st me beg; this begging is not strange.   211

ROSALINE

Play, music, then. Nay, you must do it soon.

Not yet. *[Music plays.]* No dance! Thus change I like the 213
    moon.

KING

Will you not dance? How come you thus estranged?

ROSALINE

You took the moon at full, but now she's changed.

KING

Yet still she is the moon, and I the man.   216

The music plays; vouchsafe some motion to it.   217

ROSALINE

Our ears vouchsafe it.

KING   But your legs should do it.

ROSALINE

Since you are strangers and come here by chance,

We'll not be nice: take hands – we will not dance.   220

KING

Why take we hands then?

ROSALINE   Only to part friends.

Curtsy, sweet hearts, and so the measure ends.

KING

More measure of this measure! Be not nice.   223

ROSALINE

We can afford no more at such a price.

KING

Price you yourselves. What buys your company?

---

209 *moonshine . . . water* i.e., nothing at all   **210** *change* round in a dance
(with a play on "change of the moon")   **211** *not strange* not foreign (even
though begged by Muscovites)   **213** *Not . . . dance* (she abruptly revokes her
consent)   **216** *man* i.e., man in the moon (a line rhyming with "man" may
have been lost)   **217** *motion* response   **220** *nice* coy   **223** *More measure* i.e.,
a greater quantity

ROSALINE
   Your absence only.
KING   That can never be.
ROSALINE
   Then cannot we be bought; and so adieu –
228   Twice to your visor, and half once to you.
KING
   If you deny to dance, let's hold more chat.
ROSALINE
230   In private then.
KING   I am best pleased with that.
     [They converse apart.]
BEROWNE   *[To the Princess, taking her for Rosaline]*
   White-handed mistress, one sweet word with thee.
PRINCESS   *[As Rosaline]*
   Honey, and milk, and sugar – there is three.
BEROWNE
233   Nay then, two treys, an if you grow so nice,
234   Metheglin, wort, and malmsey – well run, dice!
   There's half a dozen sweets.
PRINCESS   Seventh sweet, adieu.
236   Since you can cog, I'll play no more with you.
BEROWNE
   One word in secret.
PRINCESS   Let it not be sweet.
BEROWNE
238   Thou grievest my gall.
PRINCESS   Gall! Bitter.
BEROWNE   Therefore meet.
     [They converse apart.]
DUMAINE   *[To Maria, taking her for Katherine]*
   Will you vouchsafe with me to change a word?

---

228 *visor* mask **233** *two treys* i.e., I'll double your "trey" with three more words; *an if* if **234** *Metheglin* Welsh drink brewed from honey; *wort* unfermented or "sweet" beer; *malmsey* sweet wine **236** *cog* cheat **238** *gall* (Berowne means "sore place"; the princess mockingly takes it as "bile"); *meet* appropriate

MARIA   *[As Katherine]*
Name it.   240
DUMAINE   Fair lady –
MARIA   Say you so? Fair lord.
Take that for your "fair lady."
DUMAINE   Please it you,
As much in private, and I'll bid adieu.
   [They converse apart.]
KATHERINE   *[As Maria]*
What, was your vizard made without a tongue?   243
LONGAVILLE
I know the reason, lady, why you ask.
KATHERINE
O for your reason! Quickly, sir; I long.
LONGAVILLE
You have a double tongue within your mask   246
And would afford my speechless vizard half.
KATHERINE
"Veal," quoth the Dutchman. Is not "veal" a calf?   248
LONGAVILLE
A calf, fair lady?
KATHERINE   No, a fair lord calf.
LONGAVILLE
Let's part the word.   250
KATHERINE   No, I'll not be your half:
Take all and wean it – it may prove an ox.   251
LONGAVILLE
Look how you butt yourself in these sharp mocks.   252
Will you give horns, chaste lady? Do not so.   253
KATHERINE
Then die a calf before your horns do grow.
LONGAVILLE
One word in private with you ere I die.

---

243 *vizard* mask   246 i.e., you are masked and deceptive   248 *Veal* i.e.,
"well" in Dutch dialect (with play on the last syllable of "Longaville" and on
"veil" – the vizard – as well as "veal" – calf); *calf* dunce   250 *half* (of what
you are; your wife – "better half")   251 *wean* i.e., raise   252 *butt* injure,
cast aspersions upon   253 *give horns* i.e., prove an unfaithful wife

KATHERINE
 Bleat softly then. The butcher hears you cry.
 [They converse apart.]
BOYET
 The tongues of mocking wenches are as keen
  As is the razor's edge invisible,
 Cutting a smaller hair than may be seen;
260 Above the sense of sense, so sensible
261 Seemeth their conference, their conceits have wings
 Fleeter than arrows, bullets, wind, thought, swifter
  things.
ROSALINE
 Not one word more, my maids! Break off, break off.
BEROWNE
264 By heaven, all dry-beaten with pure scoff!
KING
 Farewell, mad wenches. You have simple wits.
     Exeunt [King, Lords, and Blackamoors].
 [The Ladies unmask.]
PRINCESS
 Twenty adieus, my frozen Muscovites.
 Are these the breed of wits so wondered at?
BOYET
 Tapers they are, with your sweet breaths puffed out.
ROSALINE
269 Well-liking wits they have, gross, gross, fat, fat.
PRINCESS
270 O poverty in wit, kingly-poor flout!
 Will they not, think you, hang themselves tonight?
  Or ever but in vizards show their faces?
 This pert Berowne was out of count'nance quite.
ROSALINE
 They were all in lamentable cases.

---

260 *sense of* i.e., reach of; *sensible* sensitive 261 *conference* conversation; *conceits* fancies 264 *dry-beaten* clubbed, bruised 269 *Well-liking* ready for market, fat (as in "fat-headed") 270 *kingly-poor* (a play on preceding *liking* – i.e., like king, kinglike, kingly); *flout* gibe

The king was weeping-ripe for a good word.   275
PRINCESS
     Berowne did swear himself out of all suit.   276
MARIA
     Dumaine was at my service, and his sword:
     "Non point," quoth I; my servant straight was mute.   278
KATHERINE
     Lord Longaville said I came o'er his heart;
     And trow you what he called me?   280
PRINCESS   Qualm, perhaps.
KATHERINE
     Yes, in good faith.   281
PRINCESS   Go, sickness as thou art!
ROSALINE
     Well, better wits have worn plain statute caps.   282
     But will you hear? The king is my love sworn.
PRINCESS
     And quick Berowne hath plighted faith to me.
KATHERINE
     And Longaville was for my service born.
MARIA
     Dumaine is mine as sure as bark on tree.
BOYET
     Madam, and pretty mistresses, give ear.
     Immediately they will again be here
     In their own shapes, for it can never be
     They will digest this harsh indignity.   290
PRINCESS
     Will they return?
BOYET   They will, they will, God knows,
     And leap for joy though they are lame with blows.
     Therefore change favors, and when they repair,   293

---

275 *weeping-ripe* i.e., ready to cry 276 *out . . . suit* (1) excessively, (2) un-availingly 278 *Non point* (cf. II.1.189) 280 *trow you* would you believe 281 *Go, sickness* (a play on *qualm* – pronounced "come" – in the preceding line) 282 *Well . . . statute caps* i.e., there have been cleverer people among ordinary citizens (whose headdress was regulated by statute) 293 *change favors* exchange tokens back again; *repair* i.e., repair hither, arrive

Blow like sweet roses in this summer air.

PRINCESS
How blow? how blow? Speak to be understood.

BOYET
Fair ladies, masked, are roses in their bud;
297   Dismasked, their damask sweet commixture shown,
298   Are angels vailing clouds, or roses blown.

PRINCESS
299   Avaunt, perplexity! What shall we do
300   If they return in their own shapes to woo?

ROSALINE
Good madam, if by me you'll be advised,
Let's mock them still, as well known as disguised.
Let us complain to them what fools were here,
Disguised like Muscovites in shapeless gear,
And wonder what they were, and to what end
Their shallow shows and prologue vilely penned,
And their rough carriage so ridiculous,
Should be presented at our tent to us.

BOYET
Ladies, withdraw. The gallants are at hand.

PRINCESS
310   Whip to your tents, as roes run o'er the land.
                    Exeunt [Princess and Ladies].
        Enter the King and the rest [of the Lords, undisguised].

KING
Fair sir, God save you. Where's the princess?

BOYET
Gone to her tent. Please it your majesty
Command me any service to her thither?

KING
That she vouchsafe me audience for one word.

BOYET
I will, and so will she, I know, my lord.   *Exit.*

---

297 *damask* i.e., mingled red-and-white complexion   298 *vailing* shedding;
blown i.e., full-blown   299 *Avaunt, perplexity* i.e., away with riddling   310
roes deer

BEROWNE

This fellow pecks up wit, as pigeons peas,
And utters it again when God doth please.   317
He is wit's peddlar, and retails his wares
At wakes and wassails, meetings, markets, fairs;   319
And we that sell by gross, the Lord doth know,   320
Have not the grace to grace it with such show.
This gallant pins the wenches on his sleeve.
Had he been Adam, he had tempted Eve.
A can carve too, and lisp. Why, this is he   324
That kissed his hand away in courtesy.
This is the ape of form, monsieur the nice,   326
That, when he plays at tables, chides the dice   327
In honorable terms. Nay, he can sing   328
A mean most meanly, and in ushering   329
Mend him who can. The ladies call him sweet.   330
The stairs, as he treads on them, kiss his feet.
This is the flower that smiles on every one,
To show his teeth as white as whalès bone;   333
And consciences that will not die in debt
Pay him the due of "honey-tongued Boyet."

KING

A blister on his sweet tongue, with my heart,
That put Armado's page out of his part!
    Enter the Ladies [with Boyet].

BEROWNE

See where it comes! Behavior, what wert thou,   338
Till this madman showed thee? and what art thou now?   339

KING

All hail, sweet madam, and fair time of day.   340

PRINCESS

"Fair" in "all hail" is foul, as I conceive.   341

---

317 *utters* issues, vends   319 *wakes* night revels; *wassails* drinking sessions
320 *by gross* wholesale   324 *A* he; *carve* act courtly   326 *nice* foppish   327
tables i.e., backgammon   328 *honorable* polite   329 *mean* an "in-between"
vocal part; *ushering* i.e., playing the groom or gentleman-in-waiting   333
whalès bone walrus ivory   338 *Behavior* i.e., fine manners   339 *madman*
wag, madcap   341 *all . . . foul* i.e., a fall of hail means foul weather

KING
     Construe my speeches better, if you may.
PRINCESS
     Then wish me better – I will give you leave.
KING
     We came to visit you, and purpose now
          To lead you to our court. Vouchsafe it then.
PRINCESS
346 This field shall hold me, and so hold your vow.
          Nor God nor I delights in perjured men.
KING
     Rebuke me not for that which you provoke.
349   The virtue of your eye must break my oath.
PRINCESS
350 You nickname virtue. "Vice" you should have spoke,
          For virtue's office never breaks men's troth.
     Now, by my maiden honor, yet as pure
          As the unsullied lily, I protest,
     A world of torments though I should endure,
          I would not yield to be your house's guest,
356 So much I hate a breaking cause to be
          Of heavenly oaths, vowed with integrity.
KING
     O, you have lived in desolation here,
          Unseen, unvisited, much to our shame.
PRINCESS
360 Not so, my lord. It is not so, I swear.
          We have had pastimes here and pleasant game.
362 A mess of Russians left us but of late.
KING
          How, madam? Russians?
PRINCESS   Ay, in truth, my lord,
     Trim gallants, full of courtship and of state.

---

346 *so hold* so uphold   349 *virtue* power (with quibble following)   350
nickname miscall   356 *breaking cause* i.e., cause of breaking   362 *mess*
group of four

ROSALINE
    Madam, speak true. It is not so, my lord.
My lady, to the manner of the days,   366
In courtesy gives undeserving praise.
We four indeed confronted were with four
In Russian habit. Here they stayed an hour
And talked apace; and in that hour, my lord,   370
They did not bless us with one happy word.   371
I dare not call them fools; but this I think,
When they are thirsty, fools would fain have drink.

BEROWNE
    This jest is dry to me. Gentle sweet,   374
Your wits makes wise things foolish. When we greet   375
With eyes best seeing heaven's fiery eye,
By light we lose light. Your capacity
Is of that nature that to your huge store
Wise things seem foolish and rich things but poor.

ROSALINE
    This proves you wise and rich, for in my eye –   380

BEROWNE
    I am a fool and full of poverty.

ROSALINE
    But that you take what doth to you belong,
It were a fault to snatch words from my tongue.

BEROWNE
    O, I am yours, and all that I possess.

ROSALINE
    All the fool mine?

BEROWNE   I cannot give you less.

ROSALINE
    Which of the vizards was it that you wore?

BEROWNE
    Where? when? what vizard? Why demand you this?

---

366 *to* in   **371** *happy* apt   **374** *dry* tart   **375** *Your wits* i.e., the greatness of
your wit; *foolish* i.e., seem foolish in comparison   **375–77** *When . . . lose
light* i.e., the power of the sun dims even the keenest sight

ROSALINE

388   There, then, that vizard, that superfluous case
    That hid the worse, and showed the better face.

KING

390   We were descried. They'll mock us now downright.

DUMAINE

    Let us confess, and turn it to a jest.

PRINCESS

392   Amazed, my lord? Why looks your highness sad?

ROSALINE

    Help! Hold his brows! He'll swoon. Why look you pale?
    Seasick, I think, coming from Muscovy.

BEROWNE

    Thus pour the stars down plagues for perjury.
        Can any face of brass hold longer out?
    Here stand I, lady, dart thy skill at me.
        Bruise me with scorn, confound me with a flout,
    Thrust thy sharp wit quite through my ignorance,

400   Cut me to pieces with thy keen conceit;

401   And I will wish thee never more to dance,

402   Nor never more in Russian habit wait.
    O, never will I trust to speeches penned,
        Nor to the motion of a schoolboy's tongue,

405   Nor never come in vizard to my friend,

406   Nor woo in rhyme, like a blind harper's song.

407   Taffeta phrases, silken terms precise,

408   Three-piled hyperboles, spruce affectation,

409   Figures pedantical – these summer flies

410   Have blown me full of maggot ostentation.
    I do forswear them; and I here protest
        By this white glove (how white the hand, God knows)
    Henceforth my wooing mind shall be expressed

---

388 *case* covering   392 *Amazed* confused   400 *conceit* fancy, ingenuity
401 *wish* invite   402 *wait* attend   405 *friend* sweetheart   406 *blind*
harper's i.e., performing street singer's   407 *precise* i.e., finely discriminated,
as in word-splitting   408 *Three-piled* deep-piled (as in richest velvet); *spruce*
jaunty   409 *Figures* figures of speech   410 *blown* laid eggs on

　　In russet yeas and honest kersey noes.　　　　　　414
　　And to begin, wench – so God help me, law! –　　415
　　My love to thee is sound, sans crack or flaw.　　416
ROSALINE
　　Sans "sans," I pray you.　　　　　　　　　　　　417
BEROWNE　　　　　　　　　Yet I have a trick
　　Of the old rage. Bear with me, I am sick.　　　　418
　　I'll leave it by degrees. Soft, let us see –
　　Write "Lord have mercy on us" on those three.　　420
　　They are infected, in their hearts it lies;
　　They have the plague, and caught it of your eyes.
　　These lords are visited; you are not free,　　　　423
　　For the Lord's tokens on you do I see.　　　　　　424
PRINCESS
　　No, they are free that gave these tokens to us.　　425
BEROWNE
　　Our states are forfeit. Seek not to undo us.　　　426
ROSALINE
　　It is not so, for how can this be true,
　　That you stand forfeit, being those that sue?　　428
BEROWNE
　　Peace! for I will not have to do with you.
ROSALINE
　　Nor shall not if I do as I intend.　　　　　　　　*430*
BEROWNE　　*[To the other men]*
　　Speak for yourselves. My wit is at an end.
KING
　　Teach us, sweet madam, for our rude transgression
　　Some fair excuse.
PRINCESS　　　　　　　The fairest is confession.

---

414 *russet* homespun; *kersey* woolen cloth　415 *law* (a "homespun" exple-
tive)　416 *sans* without　417 *Yet* still; *trick* trace　418 *rage* fever　420
Lord . . . us (the words posted on houses containing victims of the plague)
423 *visited* infected; *free* i.e., free of infection　424 *tokens* plague spots　425
free i.e., liberal (with *tokens* taken up in the sense of "gifts")　426 *states* estates; *forfeit* subject to confiscation; *undo* ruin　428 *sue* i.e., instead of the
ones sued

Were you not here but even now disguised?

KING
435   Madam, I was.

PRINCESS   And were you well advised?

KING
I was, fair madam.

PRINCESS   When you then were here,
What did you whisper in your lady's ear?

KING
That more than all the world I did respect her.

PRINCESS
When she shall challenge this, you will reject her.

KING
440   Upon mine honor, no.

PRINCESS   Peace, peace, forbear!
441   Your oath once broke, you force not to forswear.

KING
Despise me when I break this oath of mine.

PRINCESS
I will, and therefore keep it. Rosaline,
What did the Russian whisper in your ear?

ROSALINE
Madam, he swore that he did hold me dear
As precious eyesight, and did value me
Above this world, adding thereto, moreover,
That he would wed me or else die my lover.

PRINCESS
God give thee joy of him. The noble lord
450   Most honorably doth uphold his word.

KING
What mean you, madam? By my life, my troth,
I never swore this lady such an oath.

ROSALINE
By heaven you did, and to confirm it plain
454   You gave me this, but take it, sir, again.

---

435 *well advised* rational   441 *force . . . forswear* i.e., forswear without effort
454 *this* i.e., the favor originally given the princess

KING
  My faith and this the princess I did give.
  I knew her by this jewel on her sleeve.

PRINCESS
  Pardon me, sir, this jewel did she wear,
  And Lord Berowne, I thank him, is my dear.
  What, will you have me, or your pearl again?

BEROWNE
  Neither of either; I remit both twain.   460
  I see the trick on't. Here was a consent,   461
  Knowing aforehand of our merriment,
  To dash it like a Christmas comedy.   463
  Some carrytale, some pleaseman, some slight zany,   464
  Some mumblenews, some trencher knight, some Dick   465
  That smiles his cheek in years, and knows the trick   466
  To make my lady laugh when she's disposed,
  Told our intents before, which once disclosed,
  The ladies did change favors, and then we,
  Following the signs, wooed but the sign of she.   470
  Now, to our perjury to add more terror,
  We are again forsworn, in will and error.
  Much upon this 'tis. *[To Boyet]* And might not you   473
  Forestall our sport, to make us thus untrue?
  Do not you know my lady's foot by th' squire,   475
    And laugh upon the apple of her eye?   476
  And stand between her back, sir, and the fire,
    Holding a trencher, jesting merrily?   478
  You put our page out. Go, you are allowed.   479
  Die when you will, a smock shall be your shroud.   480
  You leer upon me, do you? There's an eye   481

---

461 *consent* agreement   463 *like* i.e., as one does   464 *pleaseman* toady; *zany* clown   465 *mumblenews* gossip; *trencher knight* parasite; *Dick* low fellow   466 *in years* i.e., into the wrinkles of old age   470 *she* i.e., the mistress intended   473 *Much . . . 'tis* i.e., this is about the way of it   475 *squire* square (i.e., have her measure, know how to please her)   476 *apple* pupil (i.e., keep your pleasantries a center of her attention; an "apple-squire" was a pimp)   478 *trencher* plate   479 *out* out of his part; *allowed* i.e., a privileged fool or jester   480 *smock* petticoat   481 *leer* scowl

Wounds like a leaden sword.

BOYET   Full merrily
483   Hath this brave manège, this career, been run.

BEROWNE
484   Lo, he is tilting straight. Peace! I have done.
      Enter [Costard the] Clown.
485   Welcome, pure wit! Thou partest a fair fray.

COSTARD
      O Lord, sir, they would know
      Whether the three Worthies shall come in or no.

BEROWNE
488   What, are there but three?

COSTARD   No, sir; but it is vara fine,
489   For every one pursents three.

BEROWNE   And three times thrice is nine.

COSTARD
490   Not so, sir, under correction, sir, I hope, it is not so.
491   You cannot beg us, sir, I can assure you, sir; we know
        what we know:
      I hope, sir, three times thrice, sir –

BEROWNE   Is not nine?

COSTARD   Under correction, sir, we know whereuntil it
      doth amount.

BEROWNE   By Jove, I always took three threes for nine.

496   COSTARD   O Lord, sir, it were pity you should get your
      living by reck'ning, sir.

BEROWNE   How much is it?

COSTARD   O Lord, sir, the parties themselves, the actors,
500   sir, will show whereuntil it doth amount. For mine own
501   part, I am, as they say, but to parfect one man in one
502   poor man – Pompion the Great, sir.

BEROWNE   Art thou one of the Worthies?

---

483 *manège* gallop at full speed; *career* charge   484 *tilting straight* i.e., at his
wordplay immediately   485 *pure wit* i.e., Costard (as compared to Boyet)
488 *vara* very   489 *pursents* represents   491 *beg us* prove us fools (derived
from the practice of seeking administration of the property of the mentally
ill)   496 *pity* i.e., too bad if   501 *parfect* perform (malapropism)   502
Pompion pumpkin

COSTARD   It pleased them to think me worthy of Pompey the Great. For mine own part, I know not the degree of the Worthy, but I am to stand for him.

BEROWNE   Go, bid them prepare.

COSTARD
We will turn it finely off, sir, we will take some care.   *Exit.*

KING
Berowne, they will shame us. Let them not approach.

BEROWNE
We are shame-proof, my lord, and 'tis some policy   510
To have one show worse than the king's and his company.

KING
I say they shall not come.

PRINCESS
Nay, my good lord, let me o'errule you now.
That sport best pleases that doth least know how,
Where zeal strives to content, and the contents   515
Dies in the zeal of that which it presents.   516
Their form confounded makes most form in mirth   517
When great things laboring perish in their birth.

BEROWNE
A right description of our sport, my lord.   519
   Enter [Armado the] Braggart.

ARMADO   Anointed, I implore so much expense of thy   520
royal sweet breath as will utter a brace of words.
   [Converses with the King and delivers a paper to him.]

PRINCESS   Doth this man serve God?

BEROWNE   Why ask you?

PRINCESS   A speaks not like a man of God his making.

ARMADO   That is all one, my fair, sweet, honey monarch,
for, I protest, the schoolmaster is exceeding fantastical –
too-too vain, too-too vain – but we will put it, as they

---

510 *policy* good policy   515 *contents* substance   516 *of that . . . presents* i.e.,
of the performance that presents this substance   517 *form confounded* i.e.,
ruined artistry; *most form* i.e., superior artistry   519 *right* exact; *our sport* i.e.,
our show of Muscovites

528   say, to *fortuna de la guerra.* I wish you the peace of mind,
529   most royal couplement!   *Exit.*
530   KING   Here is like to be a good presence of Worthies. He
       presents Hector of Troy; the swain, Pompey the Great;
       the parish curate, Alexander; Armado's page, Hercules;
       the pedant, Judas Maccabaeus:
       And if these four Worthies in their first show thrive,
535   These four will change habits and present the other
       five.
       BEROWNE   There is five in the first show.
       KING   You are deceivèd, 'tis not so.
       BEROWNE
538   The pedant, the braggart, the hedge-priest, the fool,
       and the boy –
539   Abate throw at novum, and the whole world again
540   Cannot pick out five such, take each one in his vein.
       KING
       The ship is under sail, and here she comes amain.
            Enter [Costard armed, for] Pompey.
       COSTARD
       I Pompey am –
       BOYET   You lie, you are not he.
       COSTARD
543   I Pompey am –
       BOYET   With leopard's head on knee.
       BEROWNE
       Well said, old mocker. I must needs be friends with
       thee.
       COSTARD
       I Pompey am, Pompey surnamed the Big –
       DUMAINE   The "Great."
       COSTARD   It is "Great," sir –

---

528 *fortuna . . . guerra* fortunes of war   **529** *couplement* couple   **530** *presence* appearance, showing   **535** *habits* costumes   **538** *hedge-priest* (term of contempt for illiterate clergyman with no regular stipend)   **539** *Abate* barring; *throw at novum* lucky throw (in the dice game of novum or nines)   **540** *vein* i.e., characteristic manner   **543** *leopard's* (a reference to the insignia of Pompey, here presumably worn on the knee)

Pompey surnamed the Great;
That oft in field, with targe and shield, did make my foe to   548
  sweat.
And traveling along this coast, I here am come by chance,
And lay my arms before the legs of this sweet lass of France.   550
If your ladyship would say, "Thanks, Pompey," I had
  done.

PRINCESS   Great thanks, great Pompey.   552
COSTARD   'Tis not so much worth; but I hope I was per-   553
  fect. I made a little fault in "Great."
BEROWNE   My hat to a halfpenny, Pompey proves the
  best Worthy.
  [Costard stands aside.] Enter [Nathaniel the] Curate,
  for Alexander.

NATHANIEL
  When in the world I lived, I was the world's commander;
    By east, west, north, and south, I spread my conquering
      might;
  My scutcheon plain declares that I am Alisander –
BOYET
    Your nose says, no, you are not; for it stands too   560
      right.
BEROWNE
    Your nose smells "no" in this, most tender-smelling
      knight.
PRINCESS
  The conqueror is dismayed. Proceed, good Alexander.
NATHANIEL
  When in the world I lived, I was the world's commander –
BOYET   Most true, 'tis right – you were so, Alisander.
BEROWNE   *[To Costard]* Pompey the Great –
COSTARD   Your servant, and Costard.
BEROWNE   Take away the conqueror, take away Al-
  isander.

---

548 *targe* shield   552 **s.p.** (Q gives "Lady"; either Shakespeare's error, or
Costard is kneeling to the wrong woman)   553 *perfect* word perfect   560
right (a reference to Alexander's wry neck, which inclined his head to the left)

COSTARD *[To Nathaniel]* O, sir, you have overthrown
570   Alisander the conqueror! You will be scraped out of the
571   painted cloth for this. Your lion that holds his poleax
      sitting on a closestool will be given to Ajax. He will be
      the ninth Worthy. A conqueror, and afeard to speak?
      Run away for shame, Alisander. *[Exit Nathaniel.]*
      There, an't shall please you, a foolish mild man, an
      honest man, look you, and soon dashed. He is a mar-
      velous good neighbor, faith, and a very good bowler,
      but for Alisander – alas, you see how 'tis – a little
579   o'erparted. But there are Worthies a-coming will speak
580   their mind in some other sort.
PRINCESS   Stand aside, good Pompey.
      Enter [Holofernes the] Pedant, for Judas, and [Moth]
      the Boy, for Hercules.
HOLOFERNES
582   Great Hercules is presented by this imp,
583   Whose club killed Cerberus, that three-headed *canus;*
      And when he was a babe, a child, a shrimp,
585   Thus did he strangle serpents in his *manus.*
586   *Quoniam* he seemeth in minority,
587   *Ergo* I come with this apology.
588   Keep some state in thy exit, and vanish.   *Exit [Moth].*
      Judas I am –
590 DUMAINE   A Judas?
HOLOFERNES   Not Iscariot, sir.
592   Judas I am, yclepèd Maccabaeus.
593 DUMAINE   Judas Maccabaeus clipped is plain Judas.
594 BEROWNE   A kissing traitor. How, art thou proved Judas?

---

571 *painted cloth* wall hanging picturing the Nine Worthies 571–74
lion . . . closestool (Alexander's insignia pictured a lion seated in a chair holding a battleax; the "closestool" [= a toilet] will be given to Ajax [= "a jakes," a
privy])   579 *o'erparted* i.e., given too hard a role   582 *imp* boy   583 *canus*
dog (*canis*)   585 *manus* hands   586 *Quoniam* since   587 *Ergo* therefore
588 *state* dignity   590 *A Judas* i.e., traitor   592 *yclepèd* called   593 *clipped*
shortened   594 *kissing traitor* (because he betrayed Jesus with a kiss, punning on "clipped," "embraced"); *How* how now

HOLOFERNES
  Judas I am –
DUMAINE The more shame for you, Judas.
HOLOFERNES What mean you, sir?
BOYET To make Judas hang himself.
HOLOFERNES Begin, sir, you are my elder.   599
BEROWNE Well followed: Judas was hanged on an elder.   600
HOLOFERNES I will not be put out of countenance.
BEROWNE Because thou hast no face.
HOLOFERNES What is this?
BOYET A citternhead.   604
DUMAINE The head of a bodkin.   605
BEROWNE A death's face in a ring.   606
LONGAVILLE The face of an old Roman coin, scarce seen.   607
BOYET The pommel of Caesar's falchion.   608
DUMAINE The carved-bone face on a flask.   609
BEROWNE Saint George's half-cheek in a brooch.   610
DUMAINE Ay, and in a brooch of lead.   611
BEROWNE
  Ay, and worn in the cap of a toothdrawer.
  And now forward, for we have put thee in counte-   613
    nance.
HOLOFERNES You have put me out of countenance.
BEROWNE False. We have given thee faces.
HOLOFERNES But you have outfaced them all.   616
BEROWNE An thou wert a lion, we would do so.
BOYET
  Therefore as he is an ass, let him go.   618
  And so adieu, sweet Jude. Nay, why dost thou stay?

---

599 *you . . . elder* i.e., you are so wise   600 (traditionally, Judas was held to
have hanged himself on an elder tree)   604 *cittern* cithern, guitar   605 *bodkin* small dagger   606 *face* head; *ring* (death's-head ring worn as a memento
mori)   607 *scarce seen* (because worn down)   608 *pommel* handle; *falchion*
sword   609 *flask* i.e., engraved horn flask   610 *half-cheek* profile   611–12
brooch . . . toothdrawer i.e., an inferior badge bearing insignia, possibly jaw-
bones, of an inferior occupation   613 *put . . . countenance* i.e., portrayed
you   616 *outfaced* abashed   618 *ass* (alluding to Aesop's fable of the ass in a
lion's skin whose disguise was betrayed by his ass's ears)

620 DUMAINE   For the latter end of his name.

BEROWNE
For the ass to the Jude? Give it him. Jud-as, away!

HOLOFERNES
622   This is not generous, not gentle, not humble.

BOYET
A light for Monsieur Judas! It grows dark, he may
stumble.   *[Exit Holofernes.]*

PRINCESS
Alas, poor Maccabaeus, how hath he been baited!
Enter [Armado the] Braggart [, for Hector].

625 BEROWNE   Hide thy head, Achilles! Here comes Hector
in arms.

627 DUMAINE   Though my mocks come home by me, I will
now be merry.

629 KING   Hector was but a Trojan in respect of this.

630 BOYET   But is this Hector?

631 KING   I think Hector was not so clean-timbered.

LONGAVILLE   His leg is too big for Hector's.

DUMAINE   More calf, certain.

634 BOYET   No; he is best indued in the small.

BEROWNE   This cannot be Hector.

DUMAINE   He's a god or a painter; for he makes faces.

ARMADO
637   The armipotent Mars, of lances the almighty,
Gave Hector a gift –

639 DUMAINE   A gilt nutmeg.

640 BEROWNE   A lemon.

LONGAVILLE   Stuck with cloves.

---

620 *end* i.e., "ass," backside   622 *humble* i.e., considerate, the reverse of ar-
rogant   625 *Hide . . . Achilles* i.e., beware, or skulk in your tent, Achilles
(the Greek champion who defeated the Trojan Hector)   627 *by me* to me, to
afflict me   629 *Trojan* ordinary chap; *respect of* comparison with   631
clean-timbered clean-limbed, well-built   634 *indued . . . small* endowed in
the ankle   637 *armipotent* powerful in arms   639–41 *gilt nutmeg . . . cloves*
(nutmegs, sometimes gilded, were used to flavor ale and wine, as were
lemons stuck with cloves; the latter were also valued for their scent: the jok-
ing is obscure but relates to Armado's artificiality)

DUMAINE   No, cloven.

ARMADO   Peace!

  The armipotent Mars, of lances the almighty,

  Gave Hector a gift, the heir of Ilion;   645

  A man so breathed that certain he would fight, yea   646

  From morn till night, out of his pavilion.   647

  I am that flower –

DUMAINE   That mint.

LONGAVILLE   That columbine.

ARMADO   Sweet Lord Longaville, rein thy tongue.   649

LONGAVILLE   I must rather give it the rein, for it runs 650
against Hector.

DUMAINE   Ay, and Hector's a greyhound.   652

ARMADO   The sweet warman is dead and rotten. Sweet
chucks, beat not the bones of the buried. When he
breathed, he was a man. But I will forward with my device. *[To the Princess]* Sweet royalty, bestow on me the
sense of hearing.   657

    Berowne steps forth.

PRINCESS   Speak, brave Hector, we are much delighted.

ARMADO   I do adore thy sweet grace's slipper.

BOYET   Loves her by the foot.   660

DUMAINE   He may not by the yard.   661

ARMADO

  This Hector far surmounted Hannibal –   662

COSTARD   The party is gone. Fellow Hector, she is gone. 663
She is two months on her way.

ARMADO   What meanest thou?

---

645 *Ilion* Troy   646 *so breathed* of such strong lungs, lasting power   647
pavilion jousting tent   649 *rein* curb   650–51 *runs against* (1) tilts against,
(2) races   652 *Hector's a greyhound* i.e., "Hector" is a term for a greyhound
657 **s.d.** *forth* forward (probably to stop Armado's continuing)   661 *yard*
(slang for "penis")   662 *surmounted* surpassed; *Hannibal* Carthaginian general who crossed the Alps by elephant to attack Rome   663 *The party is gone*
(Q gives this as a s.d.; it might be Armado's line, meaning "Hector is dead" –
or almost anyone's)

COSTARD   Faith, unless you play the honest Trojan, the
667   poor wench is cast away. She's quick; the child brags in
her belly already. 'Tis yours.

669   ARMADO   Dost thou infamonize me among potentates?
670   Thou shalt die.

COSTARD   Then shall Hector be whipped for Jaquenetta
that is quick by him, and hanged for Pompey that is
dead by him.

DUMAINE   Most rare Pompey!

BOYET   Renowned Pompey!

BEROWNE   Greater than great. Great, great, great Pompey! Pompey the Huge!

DUMAINE   Hector trembles.

679   BEROWNE   Pompey is moved. More Ates, more Ates! Stir
680   them on, stir them on!

DUMAINE   Hector will challenge him.

682   BEROWNE   Ay, if a have no more man's blood in his belly
than will sup a flea.

684   ARMADO   By the north pole, I do challenge thee.

685   COSTARD   I will not fight with a pole, like a northern
man. I'll slash, I'll do it by the sword. I bepray you, let
me borrow my arms again.

DUMAINE   Room for the incensed Worthies!

COSTARD   I'll do it in my shirt.

690   DUMAINE   Most resolute Pompey!

691   MOTH   Master, let me take you a buttonhole lower. Do
692   you not see, Pompey is uncasing for the combat? What
mean you? You will lose your reputation.

ARMADO   Gentlemen and soldiers, pardon me. I will not
combat in my shirt.

DUMAINE   You may not deny it. Pompey hath made the
challenge.

---

667 *quick* pregnant   669 *infamonize* infamize, slander   679 *Ates* under-
world spirits of discord   682 *a* he; *blood . . . belly* i.e., courage   684–86
(Costard as the one challenged has the right to choose weapons)   685–86
northern man (from Scotland or the north of England, probably border cattle thieves)   691 *take . . . lower* (1) take you down to your underwear, (2)
humiliate you (proverbial)   692 *uncasing* undressing

ARMADO   Sweet bloods, I both may and will.

BEROWNE   What reason have you for't?

ARMADO   The naked truth of it is, I have no shirt. I go   *700*
woolward for penance.   701

MOTH   True, and it was enjoined him in Rome for want   702
of linen; since when, I'll be sworn he wore none but a
dishclout of Jaquenetta's, and that a wears next his
heart for a favor.   705

 Enter a Messenger, Monsieur Marcadé.

MARCADÉ
God save you, madam.

PRINCESS
Welcome, Marcadé,
But that thou interrupt'st our merriment.

MARCADÉ
I am sorry, madam, for the news I bring
Is heavy in my tongue. The king your father –   *710*

PRINCESS
Dead, for my life!

MARCADÉ   Even so. My tale is told.

BEROWNE
Worthies, away! The scene begins to cloud.

ARMADO   For mine own part, I breathe free breath. I   713
have seen the day of wrong through the little hole of
discretion, and I will right myself like a soldier.

         Exeunt Worthies.

KING
How fares your majesty?

QUEEN
Boyet, prepare. I will away tonight.   717

---

701 *woolward for penance* i.e., with wool next to the skin to discipline the
flesh **702 s.p.** (Q reads "Boy," which might mean "Boyet") **705 s.d.** *Marcadé* (the name suggests a combination of Mercury, messenger of the gods
[see line 913], and a figure who mars Arcadia, the pastoral world of Navarre's
park) **713–15** *I have . . . discretion* i.e., I have caught on to the fact that I
have done wrong ("to see day through a little hole" was proverbial for "to be
no fool") **717 s.p.** (she is a princess no longer)

KING
    Madam, not so. I do beseech you, stay.
QUEEN
    Prepare, I say. I thank you, gracious lords,
720   For all your fair endeavors, and entreat,
    Out of a new-sad soul, that you vouchsafe
722   In your rich wisdom to excuse or hide
723   The liberal opposition of our spirits,
    If overboldly we have borne ourselves
725   In the converse of breath: your gentleness
726   Was guilty of it. Farewell, worthy lord.
727   A heavy heart bears not a humble tongue;
728   Excuse me so, coming too short of thanks
729   For my great suit so easily obtained.
KING
730   The extreme parts of time extremely forms
    All causes to the purpose of his speed,
732   And often, at his very loose, decides
    That which long process could not arbitrate,
734   And though the mourning brow of progeny
    Forbid the smiling courtesy of love
736   The holy suit which fain it would convince,
    Yet, since love's argument was first on foot,
    Let not the cloud of sorrow jostle it
    From what it purposed, since to wail friends lost
740   Is not by much so wholesome-profitable
    As to rejoice at friends but newly found.
QUEEN
742   I understand you not. My griefs are double.

---

722 *hide* i.e., ignore   723 *liberal* too free   725 *converse of breath* exchange of conversation; *gentleness* courtesy   726 *guilty of* responsible for   727 *humble* i.e., adapted to courtly civilities (often emended to "nimble")   728 *so* therefore   729 *suit* i.e., the property claims (which Navarre has evidently granted)   730–31 *The . . . speed* i.e., final moments enforce quick decisions   732 *his* i.e., time's; *loose* slipping away, release (archery term)   734 *progeny* i.e., child of the deceased   736 *suit . . . convince* i.e., the case it would like to make   742 *double* i.e., her failure to understand is an additional grief

BEROWNE

   Honest plain words best pierce the ear of grief;
   And by these badges understand the king.   744
   For your fair sakes have we neglected time,   745
   Played foul play with our oaths. Your beauty, ladies,
   Hath much deformed us, fashioning our humors
   Even to the opposèd end of our intents;   748
   And what in us hath seemed ridiculous –
   As love is full of unbefitting strains,   750
   All wanton as a child, skipping and vain,
   Formed by the eye and therefore, like the eye,
   Full of straying shapes, of habits and of forms,   753
   Varying in subjects as the eye doth roll
   To every varied object in his glance,
   Which parti-coated presence of loose love   756
   Put on by us, if, in your heavenly eyes,
   Have misbecomed our oaths and gravities,   758
   Those heavenly eyes that look into these faults
   Suggested us to make. Therefore, ladies,   760
   Our love being yours, the error that love makes
   Is likewise yours. We to ourselves prove false,
   By being once false for ever to be true
   To those that make us both – fair ladies, you.
   And even that falsehood, in itself a sin,
   Thus purifies itself and turns to grace.

QUEEN

   We have received your letters, full of love;
   Your favors, the ambassadors of love;
   And in our maiden council rated them   769
   At courtship, pleasant jest, and courtesy,   770
   As bombast and as lining to the time.   771

---

744 *badges* tokens, testimony   745 *neglected time* i.e., disregarded proper occasion   748 *Even . . . intents* quite contrary to our intentions   750 *strains* impulses   753 *straying* (often emended to "strange"); *habits* demeanors   756 *parti-coated presence* i.e., jesting appearance   758 *misbecomed* been unbecoming to   760 *Suggested . . . make* tempted us to make them   769 *rated* evaluated   770 *At* at no more than   771 *bombast . . . time* i.e., way to fill in time; *bombast, lining* padding

772 But more devout than this in our respects
Have we not been, and therefore met your loves
In their own fashion, like a merriment.
DUMAINE
Our letters, madam, showed much more than jest.
LONGAVILLE
776 So did our looks.
ROSALINE   We did not quote them so.
KING
Now, at the latest minute of the hour,
Grant us your loves.
QUEEN   A time, methinks, too short
To make a world-without-end bargain in.
780 No, no, my lord, your grace is perjured much,
781 Full of dear guiltiness; and therefore this –
782 If for my love (as there is no such cause)
783 You will do aught, this shall you do for me:
Your oath I will not trust, but go with speed
To some forlorn and naked hermitage,
Remote from all the pleasures of the world;
787 There stay until the twelve celestial signs
Have brought about the annual reckoning.
If this austere insociable life
790 Change not your offer made in heat of blood,
791 If frosts and fasts, hard lodging and thin weeds,
Nip not the gaudy blossoms of your love,
793 But that it bear this trial and last love,
Then, at the expiration of the year,
795 Come challenge me, challenge me by these deserts,
And, by this virgin palm now kissing thine,
I will be thine, and till that instance, shut
My woeful self up in a mourning house,
Raining the tears of lamentation

---

772 *devout* serious; *respects* consideration   776 *quote* interpret   781 *dear* grievous   782 *such cause* i.e., reason why you should   783 *aught* anything (i.e., everything)   787 *signs* i.e., of the zodiac (the months)   791 *weeds* garments   793 *last* remain   795 *these deserts* i.e., demonstrated merit

For the remembrance of my father's death.   *800*
If this thou do deny, let our hands part,
Neither intitled in the other's heart.

KING
If this, or more than this, I would deny,
  To flatter up these powers of mine with rest,   *804*
The sudden hand of death close up mine eye!
    Hence hermit then – my heart is in thy breast.   *806*
    [They talk apart.]

[BEROWNE
  And what to me, my love? and what to me?

ROSALINE
  You must be purgèd too; your sins are racked,
  You are attaint with faults and perjury;
  Therefore, if you my favor mean to get,
  A twelvemonth shall you spend, and never rest,
  But seek the weary beds of people sick.]

DUMAINE   *[To Katherine]*
  But what to me, my love? but what to me?
  A wife?

KATHERINE   A beard, fair health, and honesty;
  With threefold love I wish you all these three.

DUMAINE
  O, shall I say "I thank you, gentle wife"?   *810*

KATHERINE
  Not so, my lord. A twelvemonth and a day
  I'll mark no words that smooth-faced wooers say.
  Come when the king doth to my lady come;
  Then, if I have much love, I'll give you some.

DUMAINE
  I'll serve thee true and faithfully till then.

KATHERINE
  Yet swear not, lest ye be forsworn again.
    [They talk apart.]

---

804 *flatter up* pamper 806 *hermit* i.e., as a hermit **806.1–806.6**
BEROWNE . . . sick (probably an undeleted first version of ll. 821–38) **806.2**
racked stretched out (some editors emend to "rank")

LONGAVILLE
    What says Maria?
MARIA   At the twelvemonth's end
    I'll change my black gown for a faithful friend.
LONGAVILLE
819 I'll stay with patience, but the time is long.
MARIA
820 The liker you – few taller are so young.
        [They talk apart.]
BEROWNE
    Studies my lady? Mistress, look on me.
    Behold the window of my heart, mine eye,
    What humble suit attends thy answer there.
    Impose some service on me for thy love.
ROSALINE
    Oft have I heard of you, my Lord Berowne,
    Before I saw you, and the world's large tongue
    Proclaims you for a man replete with mocks,
828 Full of comparisons and wounding flouts,
829 Which you on all estates will execute
830 That lie within the mercy of your wit.
    To weed this wormwood from your fruitful brain,
    And therewithal to win me, if you please –
    Without the which I am not to be won –
    You shall this twelvemonth term from day to day
    Visit the speechless sick, and still converse
    With groaning wretches; and your task shall be
    With all the fierce endeavor of your wit
838 To enforce the painèd impotent to smile.
BEROWNE
    To move wild laughter in the throat of death?
840 It cannot be, it is impossible:
    Mirth cannot move a soul in agony.

----

819 *stay* wait   820 *liker* more like   828 *comparisons* i.e., similes of a derisive
sort; *flouts* gibes   829 *estates* sorts of people   838 *painèd impotent* those
prostrated by suffering

ROSALINE
  Why, that's the way to choke a gibing spirit,
  Whose influence is begot of that loose grace   843
  Which shallow laughing hearers give to fools.
  A jest's prosperity lies in the ear
  Of him that hears it, never in the tongue
  Of him that makes it. Then, if sickly ears,
  Deafed with the clamors of their own dear groans,   848
  Will hear your idle scorns, continue then,
  And I will have you and that fault withal.   850
  But if they will not, throw away that spirit,
  And I shall find you empty of that fault,
  Right joyful of your reformation.
BEROWNE
  A twelvemonth? Well, befall what will befall,
  I'll jest a twelvemonth in an hospital.
QUEEN   *[To the King]*
  Ay, sweet my lord, and so I take my leave.
KING
  No, madam, we will bring you on your way.
BEROWNE
  Our wooing doth not end like an old play:
  Jack hath not Jill. These ladies' courtesy   859
  Might well have made our sport a comedy.   *860*
KING
  Come, sir, it wants a twelvemonth and a day,
  And then 'twill end.
BEROWNE   That's too long for a play.
    Enter [Armado the] Braggart.
ARMADO   Sweet majesty, vouchsafe me.
QUEEN   Was not that Hector?
DUMAINE   The worthy knight of Troy.
ARMADO   I will kiss thy royal finger and take leave. I am
  a votary; I have vowed to Jaquenetta to hold the plow 867

---

843 *loose grace* slack approval 848 *dear* grievous 850 *withal* in addition
859 *courtesy* polite compliance 867 *hold the plow* i.e., farm

for her sweet love three year. But, most esteemed great-
869   ness, will you hear the dialogue that the two learned
870   men have compiled in praise of the owl and the
cuckoo? It should have followed in the end of our show.
KING   Call them forth quickly; we will do so.
ARMADO   Holla! approach.

Enter all [i.e., Holofernes, Nathaniel, Costard, Dull,
Jaquenetta, and others].

This side is Hiems, Winter; this Ver, the Spring: the
one maintained by the owl, th' other by the cuckoo.
Ver, begin.

The Song.

[SPRING] *[Sings.]*
> When daisies pied and violets blue
878   >   And lady-smocks all silver-white
879   > And cuckoo-buds of yellow hue
880   >   Do paint the meadows with delight,
> The cuckoo then, on every tree,
> Mocks married men, for thus sings he:
> > "Cuckoo!
884   > Cuckoo, cuckoo!" O, word of fear,
> Unpleasing to a married ear!

886   > When shepherds pipe on oaten straws,
887   >   And merry larks are plowmen's clocks,
888   > When turtles tread, and rooks, and daws,
>   And maidens bleach their summer smocks,
890   > The cuckoo then, on every tree,
> Mocks married men, for thus sings he:
> > "Cuckoo!
> Cuckoo, cuckoo!" O, word of fear,
> Unpleasing to a married ear!

---

869 *dialogue* debate **878** *lady-smocks* cuckoo-flowers (*Cardamine pratensis*)
879 *cuckoo-buds* (probably) buttercups (*Ranunculus bulbosus*) **884** *word of*
fear (because it sounds like "cuckold") **886** *oaten straws* pipes made of oat
reeds **887** *plowmen's clocks* (since plowmen "rise with the lark") **888** *turtles*
tread turtledoves mate; *daws* jackdaws

WINTER *[Sings.]*

    When icicles hang by the wall,
        And Dick the shepherd blows his nail,   896
    And Tom bears logs into the hall,
        And milk comes frozen home in pail,
    When blood is nipped, and ways be foul,
    Then nightly sings the staring owl: 900
                  "Tu-who!
    Tu-whit, tu-who!" – a merry note,
    While greasy Joan doth keel the pot.   903

    When all aloud the wind doth blow,
        And coughing drowns the parson's saw,   905
    And birds sit brooding in the snow,
        And Marian's nose looks red and raw,
    When roasted crabs hiss in the bowl,   908
    Then nightly sings the staring owl:
                  "Tu-who!   *910*
    Tu-whit, tu-who!" – a merry note,
    While greasy Joan doth keel the pot.

ARMADO   The words of Mercury are harsh after the 913
songs of Apollo. You, that way: we, this way.   914
                                Exeunt omnes.

---

896 *nail* fingernails   903 *keel* stir and skim (to prevent boiling over)   **905** *saw* maxim   **908** *crabs* crab apples   **913** *Mercury* messenger of the gods (suggesting Marcadé's message; but Mercury was also linked to scholarship, and it may suggest the work the men must do after the end of the play)   **914** *Apollo* Greek god associated with song and beauty; *You* (either the princess's party leaving the king's group or the theater audience leaving the actors; less probably it could mark the division of aristocrats from lower-class figures or Spring from Winter)

The distinguished Pelican Shakespeare series, newly revised
to be the premier choice for students, professors, and
general readers well into the 21st century